4

For Your Information

Reading and Vocabulary Skills
SECOND EDITION

KAREN BLANCHARD   CHRISTINE ROOT

TEACHER'S MANUAL
with TESTS and ANSWER KEYS

NAN CLARKE

PEARSON
Longman

For Your Information 4, Second Edition
Teacher's Manual with Tests and Answer Keys

Pearson Education, 10 Bank Street, White Plains, NY 10606

Staff credits: The people who made up the *For Your Information 4* team, representing editorial, production, design, and manufacturing, are Rhea Banker, Mindy DePalma, Christine Edmonds, Gosia Jaros-White, Laura Le Dréan, Linda Moser, Edith Pullman, Gina Dilillo, Mykan White, and Pat Wosczyk.
Cover design: MADA Design, Inc.
Text font: 11/13 Times Roman
Text composition: Laserwords

LONGMAN ON THE **WEB**

Longman.com offers online resources for teachers and students. Access our Companion Websites, our online catalog, and our local offices around the world.

Visit us at **longman.com.**

ISBN-10: 0-13-238011-0
ISBN-13: 978-013-2380119

Printed in the United States of America

CONTENTS

Scope and Sequence

UNIT	CHAPTER	READING SELECTION	READING SKILL
1 **WHAT LANGUAGES DO YOU SPEAK?**	Chapter 1	Reaping the Rewards of Learning English	Reading with a Purpose Summarizing
	Chapter 2	The Hope of Esperanto	Previewing and Predicting Summarizing
	Chapter 3	Instant Messaging: Shaping Our Lives	Using Background Knowledge Skimming for the Main Idea Identifying Facts and Opinions

abcNEWS **Video Excerpt:** The IM Code

UNIT	CHAPTER	READING SELECTION	READING SKILL
2 **DON'T WORRY, BE HAPPY**	Chapter 1	The E-Factor!	Reading with a Purpose
	Chapter 2	Happiness Is . . .	Paraphrasing
	Chapter 3	How Color Can Change Your Life	Previewing and Predicting Making Inferences Summarizing

abcNEWS **Video Excerpt:** How to Be Happy

UNIT	CHAPTER	READING SELECTION	READING SKILL
3 **HOME AND FAMILY**	Chapter 1	The House on Mango Street	Making Inferences
	Chapter 2	My House	Understanding Tone
	Chapter 3	Birth Order: What It Means for Your Kids . . . and You	Using Backgound Knowledge Paraphrasing Using Graphic Organizers: Charts Understanding Figurative Language

abcNEWS **Video Excerpt:** The Role of Birth Order in History

UNIT	CHAPTER	READING SELECTION	READING SKILL
4 **WINNING AND LOSING**	Chapter 1	Athletes as Role Models	Previewing and Predicting Making Inferences Identifying Supporting Information
	Chapter 2	Olympic Marathons, Then and Now	Reading with a Purpose Scanning for Information Recognizing Sequence Using Graphic Organizers: Making a Timeline
	Chapter 3	Helping Athletes Go for the Gold	Paraphrasing Summarizing

abcNEWS **Video Excerpt:** Barefoot Marathon

VOCABULARY SKILL	APPLICATION SKILL
Learning Synonyms	Reading an Autobiography Understanding Emoticons Writing a Journal Entry
Understanding Word Parts: The Prefixes -ant and -ent	
Learning Word Forms	
Understanding Word Parts: The Suffix -some	Reading an Interview Choosing a Title Writing a Journal Entry
Understanding Word Parts: The Prefix mis-	
Learning Idioms: Expressions about Color	
Recognizing Commonly Confused Words	Completing a Questionnaire Writing a Journal Entry
Learning Antonyms	
Learning Synonyms and Antonyms	
Understanding Word Parts: The Suffixes -ance and -ence	Reading Poetry Writing a Journal Entry
Learning Idioms: Expressions about Competition and Sports Learning Synonyms and Antonyms	
Understanding Word Parts: The Prefixes en- and em-	

Scope and Sequence

VOCABULARY SKILL	APPLICATION SKILL
Learning Synonyms and Antonyms Understanding Word Parts: The Suffix *-less* Understanding Word Parts: The Prefix *dis-*	Reading a Prescription Label Writing a Journal Entry
Learning Homonyms	
Learning Two-Word Verbs with P*ull*	Taking a Survey Writing a Journal Entry
Understanding Word Parts: The Suffix *-ist*	
Understanding Word Parts: The Prefixes *il-, ir-, im-,* and *in-*	
Learning Synonyms and Antonyms Understanding Word Parts: The Suffix *-ize* Understanding Word Parts: The Suffixes *-able* and *-ible* Understanding Word Parts: The Suffix *-ical*	Researching a Planet Academic Degree Abbreviations Writing a Journal Entry
Learning Idioms	Analyzing Ads Choosing a Title Writing a Journal Entry
Learning Synonyms and Antonyms Recognizing Commonly Confused Words	

The FYI Approach

Welcome to *For Your Information,* a reading and vocabulary skill-building series for English language learners. The FYI series is based on the premise that students are able to read at a higher level of English than they can produce. An important goal of the texts is to help students move beyond passive reading to become active, thoughtful, and confident readers of English.

Each level in the series is tailored to focus on the specific needs of students to increase their vocabulary base and to build their reading skills. In addition to comprehension and vocabulary practice activities, reading and vocabulary-building skills are presented throughout each chapter. Although FYI is a reading series, students also practice speaking, listening, and writing throughout the texts. In trademark FYI style, the tasks in all books are varied, accessible, and inviting, and they provide stimuli for frequent interaction.

The Second Edition

This popular series is now in its second edition. The book numbers have changed in the new edition and include the following levels:

For Your Information 1 Beginning
For Your Information 2 High-Beginning
For Your Information 3 Intermediate
For Your Information 4 High-Intermediate

The second edition of *For Your Information 4* features
- new and updated reading selections
- designated target vocabulary words for study and practice
- expanded activities for building reading skills
- vocabulary building skills and "word-attack" activities
- a companion DVD of ABC News excerpts on related themes, with accompanying activities
- a glossary of target vocabulary words used in the readings

Teaching *For Your Information*

COMPONENTS

Each level of the FYI series includes a student book, a teacher's manual, which includes eight unit tests, an audio CD with recordings of the readings, and a DVD of related excerpts from ABC News programs.

STUDENT BOOK

Each student book in the FYI series contains eight thematically based units. The themes have universal appeal and allow for natural recycling of vocabulary and content.

UNIT FORMAT

All units open with a page of art and activities that introduce the theme. This is followed by three chapters with one reading each, a review section called *Tie It All Together,* and a *Vocabulary Self-Test.*

UNIT INTRODUCTION

The one-page introduction to each unit provides students with opportunities to review what they already know about the topic and uses related vocabulary that they already know in English. This page always includes a visual prompt such as a photo or cartoon. Since this art sets the stage for the whole unit, make sure students use it as a springboard for discussion or vocabulary reinforcement. The page also includes several *Points to Ponder* questions designed to activate background knowledge and to provide a framework for a student-generated discussion of the theme. To this end, the questions are intended to encourage students to personalize the information and to bring their own experiences into the discussion.

THE CHAPTERS

Each unit consists of three separate chapters. Each chapter is built on a reading passage directly related to the theme of the unit. All readings are either authentic or adapted from authentic sources. The variety of sources, including magazine and newspaper articles, interviews, the Internet, and works of fiction, nonfiction, and poetry, expose students to the wide range of writing styles they may expect to encounter in their everyday lives.

Specific reading and vocabulary skills, called *Skills for Success,* are presented in each chapter. Fluent reading involves a combination of specific reading skills (e.g., predicting, skimming for main ideas, scanning for specific information, identifying main and supporting ideas, distinguishing between facts and opinions) that can be identified, practiced, and evaluated. Most second-language learners benefit from explicit instruction in these skills. This involves giving the skill a name, explaining why the skill is helpful, describing how to use the skill effectively, and providing practice in using it. The specific skills are recycled throughout the text to give students practice using them in a variety of contexts. The *Skills for Success* also include vocabulary-building strategies and "word-attack" skills, such as understanding word parts, learning synonyms and antonyms, organizing words, understanding phrasal verbs, and inferring meaning from context. In addition, general language and learning strategies (organizing information, taking notes, and making charts.) are included throughout chapters to enhance students' ability to comprehend, evaluate, and remember information. Finally, real-life skills such as using maps, reading menus, recognizing common signs and symbols, and interpreting graphs, are interspersed throughout the series.

Reflecting our philosophy that reading is an interactive process, the chapters have three main sections: *Before You Read*, *Reading*, and *After You Read.*

Before You Read

Since successful activation of background knowledge has been shown to greatly enhance the reading experience, each chapter begins with a *Before You Read* section to get students thinking about what they already know about the topic of the reading. The first activity is usually done with a partner to encourage collaborative learning. The second activity introduces the target vocabulary that students will encounter in the passage. Vocabulary words and phrases that are essential to understanding the passage are presented before the reading in order to improve students' comprehension and fluency as they read.

Reading

The reading in each chapter is related to the overall theme of the unit. This allows students to explore the theme in depth. All the reading passages were chosen with the idea that students relate better to high-interest texts that present real information.

After You Read

This section includes comprehension exercises and vocabulary practice. A variety of exercise types are used to reflect the different styles of students. Students can work alone, in pairs, or in small groups to complete these exercises. The reading comprehension exercises test recall and understanding. They often require students to employ a specific reading skill to complete the task. For example, if students have learned the skill of recognizing time order, they might be expected to number events from the reading in the correct time order.

The *Vocabulary Practice* includes several exercises. The first is designed to test word meanings in the context of the reading, and the second challenges students to use the vocabulary in new contexts. These are followed by the presentation of a specific vocabulary skill that students practice and must use in order to complete the remaining vocabulary exercises.

Talk It Over This section provides students with an opportunity to talk about the topic of the reading in pairs, small groups, or as a class. The questions are designed to motivate learners to relate the reading to their own experiences. Students are encouraged to share their opinions and to bring their own experiences into the discussion.

Expansion Activities Many chapters include an additional expansion activity that encourages students to expand on their real-life skills, such as reading help-wanted ads, using charts and graphs, and doing research. Other expansion activities are designed to allow students to interact with each other by conducting surveys, holding debates, and completing collaborative hands-on projects such as making posters, and cookbooks.

FYIs These are pieces of information related to the unit theme that are interspersed throughout the text.

Tie It All Together Each unit concludes with a section called *Tie It All Together* that returns to the general theme of the unit. This section has five parts: *Discussion, Just for Fun, Video Activity, Reader's Journal,* and *Vocabulary Self-Test.*

Discussion The discussion questions in this section are more open-ended than those in the chapters. Students should be encouraged to express their opinions about the topics they have read about. The questions can also be used for writing prompts or class debates.

Just for Fun The Just for Fun activities provide enjoyable ways for students to use the language they have learned in the unit. The activities include crossword puzzles, games, and word searches.

Video Activity The video activity is built around a short segment from ABC News that is related to the unit topic. Teachers should preview the video before showing it and create previewing questions that activate prior knowledge. Before showing the video to students, go over the meanings of the vocabulary items and discuss any additional words and expressions that may interfere with comprehension.

Reader's Journal A Reader's Journal at the end of each unit integrates reading and writing and helps students reflect on what they have read in a non-threatening format. The purpose of the writing task is to encourage students to reflect on, synthesize, and react to the ideas they have read about and discussed in the unit. Specific topics are provided as prompts for journal entries, but students are free to write about anything they want.

Vocabulary Self-Test The Vocabulary Self-Test at the end of each unit tests students on the target words presented at the beginning of each reading. Students should be encouraged to check their answers in the answer key and to monitor their own progress.

UNIT TESTS

The *Unit Tests*, which are found at the back of this Teacher's Manual, consist of readings related to each unit theme, followed by questions that test comprehension as well as reading and vocabulary skills presented in the corresponding Student Book unit. These tests should be given after work on the unit is completed.

UNIT-by-UNIT TEACHING TIPS

WHAT LANGUAGES DO YOU SPEAK?

Theme: In Unit 1, students explore topics related to the theme of language.

Readings: The reading in Chapter 1 is a newspaper article about a young girl from Korea who has accomplished some amazing feats since she came to the United States. In Chapter 2, the reading describes an artificial international language called Esperanto. The reading in Chapter 3 is an article about the popularity of instant messaging and its effects on communication.

Skills for Success: Reading with a Purpose, Summarizing, Learning Synonyms, Previewing and Predicting, The Suffixes *-ant* and *-ent*, Using Background Knowledge, Skimming for the Main Idea, Identifying Facts and Opinions, Learning Word Forms

Vocabulary:

abandoning	embraced	neglecting	sloppy
advocates	evolved	participants	submitted
alarming	exceptions	qualms	ups and downs
artificial	feat	revitalize	vision
bewildered	humiliated	risky	worthwhile
daring	multiple	rough	

Points to Ponder

- Read the introduction aloud, or ask for a volunteer to read it to the class.

- Introduce the subject of languages, and brainstorm a list of language-related words. Write the words on the board as students call them out.

- Divide the class into small groups to discuss the Points to Ponder questions on page 1. Act as a facilitator during small-group activities by walking around the room and encouraging all students to participate in the discussions.

- On the board, make a list of all the languages students in the class know.

- Discuss the similarities and differences between students' native language and English.

- Ask for volunteers to teach the class how to say several words in their native language.

Chapter 1: Reaping the Rewards of Learning English (pages 2–10)

Before You Read

- Make sure students understand the instructions for completing the chart.
- After students have discussed their choices with a partner, take a class poll to find out which three things were most difficult for them in learning English.

SKILL FOR SUCCESS: Reading with a Purpose

Explain that efficient readers use various strategies before, during, and after they read to help them understand and remember information. Tell them that there are several strategies to use before they read something. Point out that before they read something, it is helpful to set a purpose for reading. Having a purpose for reading will provide a reason to read. It helps to read with a specific goal in mind. To set a purpose, they can ask questions that they would like the reading to answer. Then, as they read the text, students look for answers to the questions.

- Hold up the following and ask questions about the purpose of reading each one:
  - a dictionary (*to find the definition of a word; to see how to spell or pronounce a word; etc.*)
  - a cookbook (*to find the recipe for a dish; to see how to bake something; etc.*)
  - a TV guide from the newspaper
  - a phone book

- Use an example from everyday life to illustrate the idea of prereading strategies. You can recycle this example when each of the other prereading skills is introduced.

  Point out that students probably already use these skills in their everyday lives. For example, have them imagine that they are visiting an amusement park such as Disney World for the first time. Before starting their day, they might take a look at a map of the park to get an idea of where the main attractions, restaurants, and restrooms are located. Or they might take a quick walk around the park to get an idea of the layout. (**Preview.**) They might also think about other amusement parks they've been to and remember which things they had the most fun doing. (**Use background knowledge.**) Then they will be in a position to **predict** which attractions they would like to visit and to make a plan for the day. (**Set a purpose.**)

- After students have completed Exercise B, invite several students to read their three questions aloud.

- Practice the pronunciation of the words and phrases on the list in Exercise C. Have students find each word or phrase on the list in the article and read the sentence. Remind them that the numbers in parentheses tell the paragraph where the word first appears. Encourage them to learn the meanings of the words and phrases before they read the article.

Reading

This reading is a newspaper article about a young girl who moved to the United States from Korea when she was fifteen years old. When she arrived, she knew almost no English, but within a few years she had graduated from high school with honors, won numerous academic awards, been accepted at Stanford University, and written a book about her experiences.

After You Read

After students complete Exercise A individually, go over the answers. Ask them to correct the false statements. Invite several students to write their corrected sentences on the board.

SKILL FOR SUCCESS: Summarizing

- Explain that a summary is a short statement that tells the important ideas of a text in the writer's own words. Point out that writing a summary will help them understand and remember the important information in the article.

- Have students work individually to complete their summaries. Then encourage them to compare their summaries with a partner's summary.

SKILL FOR SUCCESS: Learning Synonyms

EXTRA PRACTICE: Play a game called Synonym Partners. Write pairs of synonyms on index cards, one word per card. Give each student one card, and challenge them to find the classmate who has the matching synonym card. When everyone has found his or her partner, have each pair read their synonyms to the class.

Talk It Over

After the class discussion, have students work in small groups to make a poster of tips for learning a new language. Instruct them to include at least five tips on the poster. Encourage them to decorate their posters. Display the posters around the classroom.

Reading about Scientific Research

- Go over these words and phrases before students read the article.

    hard-wired   *taken over*   *tactile*   *auditory*

- Go over the answers to the questions about "The Bilingual Brain" before students write their summaries.

- After students have completed the summarizing activity, invite several students to read their summaries to the class.

EXTRA PRACTICE: Make copies of other scientific articles for students to read and summarize for homework.

Chapter 2: The Hope of Esperanto (pages 11–18)

Before You Read

SKILL FOR SUCCESS: Previewing and Predicting

- Give an explanation of previewing and predicting and explain why they are useful skills.

- Tell students that before they read something they should quickly look over, or *preview*, the material. If the text is an article or a textbook chapter, they should read the title and subtitle, section headings, words in bold print or italics, and introductions. They should also look at the pictures and graphics. Previewing is useful because it provides an idea about the topic of the text and how it is organized.

- Point out that after they have previewed an article, they will be able to make *predictions*, or guesses, about what they are going to read. Then as they read they can continue to make predictions about what will come next in the passage. Predicting before and while reading is important because it keeps students actively involved in reading, and therefore they will understand and remember more of what they read.

Reading

The article describes the artificial language Esperanto. It gives a brief history and discusses some of the benefits of an international language.

FYI: There are many good sites about Esperanto on the Internet, such as www.esperanto.net.

After You Read

After students complete Exercise A individually, go over the correct answers. Ask students to correct the false statements. Invite several students to write their corrected sentences on the board.

Summarizing

Prepare students to write a summary of the article by going over the three questions orally. Remind them to include the answers to these questions in their summaries.

SKILL FOR SUCCESS: Understanding Word Parts: The Suffixes *-ant* and *-ent*

- Give a general introduction to word parts and explain that students can improve their vocabulary skills by learning about the structure of words and how they are formed in English. Many English words are made up of several parts. They are called prefixes, roots, and suffixes. Write *informally* on the board and explain the three parts (the root, the prefix *in-*, and the suffix *-ly*).

- After students have completed the chart in Exercise C, go over the correct definitions.

Reading an Autobiography

- Ask some questions about autobiographies. Find out if any students have read an autobiography. Also ask whose autobiography they would be interested in reading.

- Go over the meanings of the words and phrases on the list. If there are other potentially difficult words in the excerpt, preview them before students read it.

Chapter 3: Instant Messaging: Shaping Our Lives (pages 19–29)

Before You Read

After students have completed the small-group work, have a class discussion about the advantages and disadvantages of communicating via e-mail. Brainstorm a list of advantages and write them on the board. Do the same with disadvantages.

SKILL FOR SUCCESS: Using Background Knowledge

- Remind students that although reading in a new language is difficult, there are ways to make it easier. One way is to think about what you already know about the subject of the reading. This is called *using background knowledge*.

- Point out to the class that the purpose of the discussion questions at the beginning of each reading is to help them begin to think about the subject of the reading. Explain that reading comprehension improves when you connect the information that you already know with new information in the text.

- Go over the list of statements in Exercise B on page 19. Make sure students understand what each sentence means before they check the ones they think are true.

SKILL FOR SUCCESS: Skimming for the Main Idea

- Remind students that people read at different speeds for different purposes. Point out that they have already practiced one technique for reading quickly—scanning. Now they are going to learn another technique for reading quickly called *skimming*.

- Stress that skimming is a valuable reading strategy to use when you are looking for the main idea of a text. When you skim, you are not concerned with details.

- Encourage students to move their eyes quickly across the lines and down the page without stopping.

Reading

This article discusses the increasing popularity of instant messaging (IM), especially among young people. It also reviews some research on the effect of IM on language and communication.

After You Read

Discuss the IM shortcuts on the chart. See if students know any other shortcuts.
This site has interesting statistics about IM:
www.pewinternet.org/pdfs/PIP_Instantmessage_Report.pdf

SKILL FOR SUCCESS: Identifying Facts and Opinions

- Point out that learning to understand the difference between facts and opinions is a valuable skill.

- Show the difference between facts and opinions. Write this sentence on the board: *English is easy to learn.* Have students raise their hands to show whether they agree or disagree with the statement. Explain that it is possible to agree or disagree with the statement because it is an opinion. It is impossible to prove whether or not the English language is easy to learn. Opinions are beliefs that cannot be proven. Then write this sentence on the board: *In one study, Baron analyzed 23 IM conversations between college students.* Explain that they can't agree or disagree with this statement because it is a fact. The number of conversations she analyzed can be counted. Facts can be checked. They can be observed, counted, and measured. Unlike an opinion, facts can be proven to be true.

- After students complete Exercise C on page 25, go over the correct answers with the whole class.

EXTRA PRACTICE: Have students work in small groups to write fact and opinion sentences. Have each group write five fact statements and five opinion statements. Give them a theme from previous units, such as animals or sports, to write about. Then invite groups to exchange statements and to identify which statements are facts and which are opinions.

SKILL FOR SUCCESS: Learning Word Forms

- Explain that many English words have verb, noun, adjective, and adverb forms. Write an example on the board of the various forms of the word *create:*

    create (verb)—She created a beautiful flower arrangement.

    creation (noun)—I am interested in the creation of the universe.

    creative (adjective)—He is a creative thinker.

    creatively (adverb)—She writes very creatively.

    Have students work in pairs to complete the word forms chart on page 26. Go over the correct answers with the whole class.

- After students complete Exercise D, invite several students to write their corrected sentences on the board.

EXTRA PRACTICE: Write sentences with errors in word forms for students to correct for homework. Here is a sample homework assignment:

Correct the sentences that have errors in word forms.

1. The committee <u>oppositions</u> the construction of a new stadium.

2. I didn't like the movie because every scene was so <u>predictably</u>.

3. We are born with a natural <u>instinctive</u> for survival.

4. This product is the result of years of <u>experimental</u>.

5. The right side of the brain controls <u>create</u> thinking.

6. A baby goes through many <u>developmentally</u> stages in the first three years of life.

7. As I read the travel brochure, I tried to <u>visual</u> the island it was describing.

8. Perry is very well read and can speak <u>intelligent</u> on a variety of subjects.

9. I agree with the <u>education</u> objectives of the school.

10. I have no <u>intend</u> of helping you with that assignment.

Read a Narrative

- Ask students some prereading questions to generate a discussion before they read the story. For example, ask:
    1. What do you do when it's late at night and you can't sleep?
    2. Do you ever go on Internet chat rooms? Which ones?

- Go over the meanings of words and phrases you think students will have difficulty with. Write the following list on the board and make sure students understand the meanings.

    impressed   *have something in common*
    intrigued   *love at first sight*

- The last sentence of the story uses the word *ironic*. Explain the meaning of *ironic*. (A situation is ironic when events turn out to be the opposite of what was expected.)

Unit 1: Tie It All Together

Discussion

Some students assume the dominant role and do most of the talking, while others may be hesitant to actively participate in small-group or pair activities. You can help shy students by encouraging them to participate. Ask them specific questions that you know they can answer. Use a lot of positive reinforcement.

Video Activity: The IM Code

Review this additional vocabulary with students before they watch the video. Write this list of IM codes on the board and have students discuss what they think each one means.

Abbreviation	(Meaning)	Abbreviation	(Meaning)
IDK	(don't know)	G2G	(Got to go)
IK	(I know)	G2R	(Got to run)
JK	(Just kidding)	?	(I have a question)
NP	(No problem)	?	(I don't understand what you mean)
OTP	(On the phone)	@TEOTD	(At the end of the day)
RUOK?	(Are you okay?)	.02	(My (or your) two cents worth)
WU?	(What's up?)	143	(I love you)
FYEO	(For your eyes only)	411	("information")
FYI	(For your information)	4EAE	(Forever and ever)
G/F	(Girlfriend)	BFF	(Best friends forever)

Reader's Journal

Tell students that they will write in their journals for ten to twenty minutes at the end of every unit. Explain that the purpose of keeping a Reader's Journal is to help them think about the ideas in the unit. Point out that they shouldn't worry about spelling, grammar, or punctuation. The goal is just to write as much as they can in English. Have them spend a few minutes thinking about the topics and ideas they read about and discussed in this unit. You may want to have them look again at the Points to Ponder and other discussion questions in the unit. Instruct students to choose a topic from the list and to answer one of the discussion questions in the unit or write about a topic of their own.

UNIT 2 — DON'T WORRY, BE HAPPY

Theme: This unit deals with the theme of feelings and moods. The main focus is on happiness.

Readings: The reading in Chapter 1 discusses enthusiasm and ways to be more enthusiastic. In Chapter 2, students read an interview with Daniel Gilbert, a psychology professor at Harvard University whose area of research is happiness. Chapter 3 describes the effect of colors on our moods.

Skills for Success: Reading with a Purpose, Understanding Word Parts: The Suffix -*some,* Paraphrasing, Understanding Word Parts: The Prefix *mis-*, Learning Idioms: Expressions about Color, Previewing and Predicting, Making Inferences, Summarizing

Vocabulary:

abundance	cynical	modest	remarkably	upbeat
adversity	fluctuate	no-brainer	savvy	wardrobe
agonize	illusions	pastels	skeptical	
awesome	illustrious	perpetual	stick to	
brilliant	irritable	persists	trite	
contagious	misguided	prevailing	turmoil	

Points to Ponder

- Read the introduction aloud, or ask for a volunteer to read it to the class.
- Take a class poll to see which three items on the list affect students' moods the most.

Chapter 1: The E-Factor! (pages 36–43)

Before You Read

- Make sure students understand the meaning of *enthusiasm* (a feeling of energetic interest in a particular subject or activity and an eagerness to be involved in it).
- After students complete Exercise B, encourage several students to read their questions to the class.

Reading

The *E* in the title "The E-Factor!" stands for *enthusiasm.* Psychologists usually focus on negative emotions such as depression and anxiety, but they are now seriously studying positive qualities such as enthusiasm. The author describes enthusiasm, gives advice on how to be a more enthusiastic person, and explains how enthusiasm can improve your life.

After You Read

After students complete the Comprehension Check, go over the answers with the whole class. Encourage students to correct their mistakes.

SKILL FOR SUCCESS: Understanding Word Parts: The Suffix -some

Explain the meaning of the suffix -some and give a few additional examples of words ending with -some:

fearsome   bothersome   threesome

Chapter 2: Happiness Is . . . (pages 44–51)

Before You Read

Go over the questions in the interview. Read each one out loud and make sure students understand what is being asked. Encourage students to restate each question in their own words.

Reading

In this interview, psychologist Dr. Daniel Gilbert discusses happiness and our sometimes misguided attempts to find it.

After You Read

After students complete the Comprehension Check individually, go over the answers. Ask students to correct the false statements. Invite several students to write their corrected sentences on the board.

SKILL FOR SUCCESS: Paraphrasing

- Read the example passage aloud. Have students read the three sample paraphrases silently and then point out that there is more than one way to paraphrase a passage.

- Give students a few minutes to paraphrase passage 1. Encourage several students to read their paraphrased versions aloud.

- If students are having trouble paraphrasing for the first time, you may want to have them work in pairs to paraphrase passages 2 and 3.

EXTRA PRACTICE: Choose some short passages from the readings in Unit 1 for students to paraphrase for homework.

SKILL FOR SUCCESS: Understanding Word Parts: The Prefix *mis-*

- Do a quick review of word parts. Explain that a prefix is a letter or letters added to the beginning of a word. Like suffixes, prefixes change the meaning of the word. Explain the meaning of the prefix *mis-*. Write the word *behave* on the board. Ask students what *behave* means (*to act in a certain way*). Then add the prefix *mis-* to the word and ask how the meaning changes. Make sure students understand that *misbehave* means *to act badly.*

- Give some additional examples of words beginning with *mis-*:
  misinterpret   misunderstand   misplace   mistreat

Before You Read

Have students use the target vocabulary words from Units 1 and 2 to make personal dictionaries. Students can work individually or in small groups to create dictionaries. Encourage them to draw pictures, alphabetize, and write sentences using the target words in context. Display the completed dictionaries around the room.

SKILL FOR SUCCESS: Previewing and Predicting

Review the steps for previewing and predicting.

1. Look at the title of the article. Point out that the title usually tells what the article is about. Ask what students think this article will be about.

2. Invite a student to read the headings aloud. Explain that the headings that appear in bold print throughout the article give more clues about the content of each section. Make sure students understand the vocabulary in the headings.

3. Have students look at the picture of a person painting a room. Have students guess why the author included this picture.

Reading

This article discusses the many ways that color affects our lives. Topics mentioned include how color affects your energy level, stress, appetite, and job.

After You Read

- Read the questions in Exercise A aloud. Have students work individually to write answers to the questions.

- Go over the correct answers. Have students work in pairs to practice asking and answering the questions.

SKILL FOR SUCCESS: Making Inferences

- Tell students that an *inference* is an educated guess based on information the author gives you.

- Point out that the ability to make inferences is a very important reading skill, but we also make inferences all the time in our everyday lives. Give an example: If your friend calls you and says, "I'm so disappointed. The game was really close until the last few seconds. Too bad we didn't make that last basket. I was sure the ball was going to go in. It seems as if we're on a losing streak." You can infer that your friend's team lost the basketball game even though she never stated it directly.

- Explain that to make good inferences when you are reading, you need to combine the clues in the reading with information you already know from your own life. Point out that this is similar to guessing the meaning of a word using context clues. They are making inferences then, too.

- After students complete Exercise B, go over the answers. Encourage students to explain how they made their inferences.

SKILL FOR SUCCESS: Learning Idioms: Expressions about Color

- Explain what idioms are. Point out that an *idiom* is an expression whose meaning you can't understand from the meanings of the individual words. Give some examples of idioms in English and ask students to give some examples from their languages.

- Point out that many idioms in English are related to color. Go over the idioms in Exercise B on page 56.

- Have students work individually or in pairs to complete the sentences.

Choose a Title

Explain that the title of a selection often expresses the main idea. You can have students skim the passage to choose the best title and then ask them to read it again more carefully. You can also have a class discussion or answer comprehension questions.

EXTRA PRACTICE:

1. You can also use this passage as a basis for more practice in paraphrasing and summarizing.

2. Play a game. Explain that like titles, newspaper headlines often express the main idea of an article.

    - Have each student clip a short newspaper or magazine article and bring it to class. Be sure they include the headline.

    - Have students cut the headline away from the article. Put all the articles in one box or basket and the headlines in another. Mix them up.

    - Have each student pick from one of the two boxes or baskets so that everyone has either a headline or an article.

    - Students mingle with each other and find the match for their headline or article. They can use questions or phrases such as "I'm looking for an article about . . . " or "I have an article about . . . and I'm looking for the headline."

    - The first two students to find a matching article and headline win.

Talk It Over

After the class discussion, make a chart on the board of what each of the colors (white, blue, black, green, red, and yellow) means in the cultures represented in your class.

Unit 2: Tie It All Together

Just for Fun

Make sure students understand how to do a crossword puzzle. Go over the Across and Down clues. Help students get started by doing one or two answers as examples. This is a good activity to do in pairs.

Video Activity: How to Be Happy

Remind students that Dr. Lykken believes you should fill your life with a steady diet of little 1 - Hap pleasures. He gives examples such as volunteering your time, playing with your dog, gardening, or, baking a lemon meringue pie. Encourage students to make a list of activities of their own 1 - Hap pleasures.

HOME AND FAMILY

Theme: In Unit 3, students explore the theme of home and family.

Readings: The reading in Chapter 1 is a story about a Mexican-American girl's move to a new house. The story in Chapter 2 deals with a boy's feelings about leaving the house he grew up in. The article in Chapter 3 discusses the impact of birth order on personality.

Skills for Success: Making Inferences, Recognizing Commonly Confused Words, Understanding Tone, Learning Antonyms, Using Background Knowledge, Paraphrasing, Using Graphic Organizers: Charts, Learning Synonyms and Antonyms, Understanding Figurative Language

Vocabulary:

absurd	dissuade	intense	rebellious	stunned
conscientious	dreamed up	landlord	refuge	sturdy
conventional	easygoing	Laundromat	sociable	swollen
crumbling	for the time being	novels	strive	
diplomatic	insignificant	peers	strong-willed	

Points to Ponder

- Divide the class into small groups to discuss the Points to Ponder questions on page 65.

- Invite students to bring in photos of their families. Encourage them to share their photos in small groups.

Chapter 1: The House on Mango Street (pages 66–71)

Before You Read

- After students discuss the questions on page 66 with a partner, invite several students to describe their homes to the class.

- Have students look at the photo of Sandra Cisneros. Tell them that she is a famous author whose stories are based on her Latino heritage.

Reading

This story is from one of Cisneros's most loved books, called *The House on Mango Street*, which is a series of stories about the life of Esperanza, an adolescent Mexican-American girl. In this story, Esperanza writes about the move with her family from the inner city to a house on Mango Street.

SKILL FOR SUCCESS: Making Inferences

- Remind students that inferences are evidence-based guesses.

- Have students work individually to choose the inferences. Then encourage them to discuss their choices with a partner.

- Go over the chart of commonly confused words on pages 70–71. Encourage students to write another sentence for each word. Invite students to read their sentences aloud or compare them in small groups.

- Have students work individually to complete Exercise C. Go over the answers with the whole class.

EXTRA PRACTICE: Write additional cloze sentences for homework.

Chapter 2: My House (pages 72–77)

Reading

In this reading, a teenager describes his feelings for the house he is about to leave.

SKILL FOR SUCCESS: Understanding Tone

- Explain that *tone* is the writer's attitude about the subject. Tone may be playful, formal, intimate, angry, serious, and so on. Point out that tone is expressed through the words and details the writer uses.

- Students may have difficulty understanding the concept of tone. Go over the meanings of words used to describe tone before they do Exercise B.

admiring	*excited*	*objective*
approving	*fearful*	*scornful*
confused	*forgiving*	*sentimental*
disappointed	*humorous*	*surprised*
embarrassed	*joyful*	*thoughtful*

SKILL FOR SUCCESS: Learning Antonyms

- Explain that antonyms are words with opposite meanings. Write several pairs of antonyms on the board as examples. Then ask students to give you antonyms for other words.

- Have students practice antonyms as a whole class. Ask students to call out words that mean the opposite of *little* (*big, large, huge,* etc.). Encourage students to call out antonyms and write one or two on the board.

EXTRA PRACTICE: Play a game called Antonym Partners. Write pairs of antonyms on index cards, one word per card. Give each student one card, and challenge students to find the classmate who has the matching antonym card. When everyone has found his or her partner, have each pair read their antonyms to the class.

Complete a Questionnaire

After students complete the questionnaire, take a class poll to find out the three most important items students chose.

Before You Read

Read the introduction aloud. Make sure students understand the meaning of *birth order*.

SKILL FOR SUCCESS: Using Background Knowledge

- Divide the class into three groups according to birth order (eldest or only child, middle, and youngest). Brainstorm a list of personality traits and write them on the board as students call them out.

- After the groups complete their lists, invite one member from each group to write the list on the board. Discuss the similarities and differences among the groups.

Reading

The article discusses the theory of birth order and describes the typical characteristics of eldest, middle and youngest children. It also discusses the differing views of several experts on the subject of birth order.

After You Read

After students complete the Comprehension Check, go over the answers with the whole class. Encourage students to correct their mistakes.

SKILL FOR SUCCESS: Using Graphic Organizers: Charts

Explain that graphic organizers are a visual representation of information. Their purpose is to help you understand, organize, and remember information from a reading. Give some examples of graphic organizers such as charts, timelines, and tables.

FYI: There are many sites on the Internet that provide templates of graphic organizers, such as, www.enchantedlearning.com/graphicorganizers.

Reading a Short Story

- Before students read the story, read the introduction aloud and ask a few questions to generate interest:
    1. Have you ever been to a desert? Where? What was it like?
    2. Do you want to travel and see the world before you settle down?

- Go over the meanings of words and phrases you think your students will have difficulty with:

    a mark of distinction   conservative   sinful   daring

- Read the story aloud, stopping at intervals to make sure students understand what the author is expressing. Encourage students to ask you questions about words and ideas they do not understand. Also, ask questions to check comprehension.

- Have students read the story a second time to themselves before they discuss the questions in small groups.

SKILL FOR SUCCESS: Understanding Figurative Language

- Explain that when a writer (or speaker) describes something through the use of unusual comparisons for effect, for interest, or to make things clearer, he or she is using *figurative language*.

- Go over the definitions of *similes, metaphors,* and *personification* and give some additional examples of each one:

    simile—My feet are as big as boats.

    metaphor—His scream was a knife piercing the air.

    personification—The feather tickled my face.

Unit 3: Tie It All Together

Discussion

Quotations and proverbs are good prompts for discussion.

FYI: This site has a huge collection of quotes and proverbs to choose from: http://www.quotationspage.com

Video Activity: The Role of Birth Order in History

Before students watch the video, give a brief explanation of the Supreme Court. You can find information at this web site: http://www.supremecourtus.gov.

UNIT 4 — WINNING AND LOSING

Theme: In this unit, students explore topics related to the theme of competition and winning and losing.

Readings: In Chapter 1, students read about how great athletes become role models for society. The reading in Chapter 2 is an article about the history of Olympic marathons. The reading in Chapter 3 is an interview with sports psychologist Robert Suinn.

Skills for Success: Previewing and Predicting, Making Inferences, Identifying Supporting Information, Understanding Word Parts: The Suffixes -*ance,* and -*ence,* Reading with a Purpose, Scanning for Information, Recognizing Sequence, Using Graphic Organizers: Making a Timeline, Learning Idioms: Expressions about Competition and Sports, Learning Synonyms and Antonyms, Paraphrasing, Summarizing, Understanding Word Parts: The Prefixes *en-* and *em-*

Vocabulary:

cheering	down the road	high-profile	running neck and neck	take in stride
collapsed	equivalent	keep their cool	spectators	triggers
consultation	exhaustion	mentors	stick with it	triumph
delight	flaws	perseverance	suspense	
distracted	get caught up in	potential	tactics	

Points to Ponder

- Read the introduction aloud.

- Have students describe the photo of Florence Griffith-Joyner. Find out if any students have heard of her and what they know about her.

FYI: You can find information about Griffith-Joyner at this site: http://www.heroism.org/class/1980/flojo.htm

Before You Read

- Explain that a role model is a person you admire and whose behavior you try to copy.

- Students may be unfamiliar with some of the athletes mentioned in the article. Give them some background information about the following athletes:

     Mickey Mantle (1931–1995), American baseball player, one of the greatest center fielders in the history of the game. Mantle hit 536 home runs in his career, the most ever by a switch-hitter (a player who bats right-handed and left-handed).

     Jackie Robinson (1919–1972), American athlete who became a civil rights icon when he broke the color barrier in Major League Baseball in 1947. Fifty years later, in recognition of his great impact on the sport and on American society, baseball officially retired Robinson's number (42) throughout the league.

     Wilma Rudolph (1940–1994), track and field athlete who was the first American woman to win three track and field gold medals at a single Olympic Games. Although she contracted double pneumonia, polio, and scarlet fever at the age of 4 and could not walk normally until the age of 11, she became an outstanding athlete and won several Olympic medals.

     Lance Armstrong (born in 1971), American cyclist, a record seven-time winner of the Tour de France, the most prestigious cycling race in the world. In 1996, Armstrong was diagnosed with cancer, which he fought and overcame, and he went on to win several more races.

     Michael Jordan (born in 1963), American professional basketball player, considered by many to be the greatest player in basketball history.

- Have students brainstorm a list of personal qualities they think make someone a good role model.

- Talk about whether students believe that athletes have a responsibility to act as role models to their fans.

SKILL FOR SUCCESS: Previewing and Predicting

- Remind students what *predicting* means and why it is helpful to make predictions before you read.

- Go over the steps for the Previewing and Predicting exercise. After students write what they think the article will be about, ask several students to tell the class their predictions.

Reading

The article explores why athletes become role models for society and the qualities they possess. The author explains that athletes are often viewed as role models because they accomplish feats many of us cannot. They also tend to demonstrate positive traits such as dedication and self-control, qualities anyone can emulate. In the face of seemingly impossible challenges, they teach us that success takes dedication, confidence, and a lot of hard work.

After You Read

Have students work individually to complete the Comprehension Check questions. Then encourage them to compare their answers with a partner's answers.

SKILL FOR SUCCESS: Making Inferences

Remind students that an *inference* is an educated guess based on information the author gives you. Have students work in pairs to choose the statements that are inferences. Go over the answers with the whole class.

SKILL FOR SUCCESS: Identifying Supporting Information

- Remind students that a paragraph usually has one main idea. Tell them that main ideas are supported with facts, reasons, and examples.

- Do the first item of Exercise C with the whole class. Make sure students understand that **b** is the main idea and that **a** and **c** provide supporting information. After students complete the exercise, go over the correct answers with the whole class.

EXTRA PRACTICE: Have students read each paragraph and then choose the sentence that could be added to support the main idea.

1. Great Smoky Mountains National Park is the home of a huge variety of plant and animal life. For example, more than 4,000 species of plants, including 130 different kinds of trees, can be found in the park. That is more plants than in any other North American national park. In addition, over 200 types of birds, 66 types of mammals, and 50 native fish species live in Great Smoky Mountains National Park. Another interesting fact is that more species of salamanders can be found there than anywhere else on our planet.

    a. There are more than 850 miles of hiking trails throughout the Great Smoky Mountains.
    b. Over 1,400 additional flowering plant species, and at least 4,000 species of nonflowering plants live in the park.
    c. The Great Smoky Mountains are among the oldest mountains in the world. They were formed about 200 or 300 million years ago.

2. The Canadian province of Saskatchewan is the largest wheat-producing area in North America and one of the largest in the world. Approximately two-fifths of Canada's farmland lies in Saskatchewan and most of the land is used to raise wheat crops. In fact, Saskatchewan produces 54 percent of Canada's wheat. In addition, huge amounts of wheat from Saskatchewan are exported to countries all over the world such as the United States, Mexico, South Korea, Iran, Brazil, Japan, and China.

    a. Saskatchewan produced its first crop of wheat in 1792, and today it is still known as Canada's breadbasket.
    b. Mining is Saskatchewan's third largest industry after oil and gas and agriculture.
    c. The name *Saskatchewan* comes from the Indian word *kisiskatchewan,* which means "swiftly flowing river."

3. Many people like to fly kites for fun, but kites have also been used for practical purposes. In 1749, for example, Alexander Wilson of Scotland used kites to carry thermometers into the sky. Benjamin Franklin also used a kite in his famous experiment in 1752 to prove that lightning is electricity. In the early 1900s the Wright Brothers used kites to test their ideas about how airplanes fly.

    a. In the late 1800s, the inventor Alexander Graham Bell used kites to study aerodynamics in hopes of inventing a flying machine.
    b. It is easy to make your own kite.
    c. The Kite Fliers Association has over 4,000 members in thirty-eight different countries.

4. Robert Louis Stevenson (1850–1894) was a Scottish author who wrote several classic works of children's literature. Children loved his adventure stories, such as *Treasure Island*, an exciting story about hunting for a pirate's treasure. Another adventure story, *Kidnapped*, takes place in Scotland in the 1700s. One of Stevenson's most loved works is called *A Child's Garden of Verses*, a collection of poems for children.

   a. Stevenson studied engineering and then law at the University of Edinburgh.

   b. Stevenson's other adventure stories include *The Black Arrow* (1888) and *The Master of Ballantrae* (1889).

   c. James Mathew Barrie, another Scottish author, wrote *Peter Pan,* one of the most famous stories in children's literature.

5. There are many interesting facts about the ostrich, the largest and strongest living bird in the world. The ostrich cannot fly, but it can run up to 40 miles per hour (65 kilometers per hour) for 30 minutes. The ostrich is the only bird that has two toes on each foot. These huge birds are about 8 feet (about 2.4 meters) tall and weigh up to 300 pounds (136 kilograms). A female ostrich can lay from 10 to 70 eggs each year. Ostriches lay the largest bird eggs. They weigh about 3 pounds (1.4 kilograms) and are about 6 to 8 inches (15 to 20 centimeters) long.

   a. Ostriches can lay more eggs at one time than any other bird—up to fifteen at one time.

   b. Like all other birds, ostriches have feathers.

   c. You can see ostriches in many zoos around the world.

SKILL FOR SUCCESS: Understanding Word Parts: The Suffixes -ance, and -ence

- Explain the meaning of the suffixes -ance and -ence. Write the word *perseverance* on the board. Circle the suffix -ance and explain that this suffix was added to the verb *persevere* to make a noun. Give some additional examples.

- After students complete Exercise C, invite several students to write their sentences on the board.

Chapter 2: Olympic Marathons, Then and Now (pages 102–111)

Before You Read

- Explain the meaning of *marathon*. (*A marathon is a running race of 42.195 kilometers.*)

- Find out if any of the students have run a marathon. Invite them to share their experiences with the class.

Reading

This article explains the origins and history of marathons and gives some interesting information about modern Olympic marathons.

After You Read

After students complete the Comprehension Check, go over the answers with the whole class. Encourage students to correct their mistakes.

SKILL FOR SUCCESS: Scanning for Information

- Explain that people read at different speeds for different purposes. Point out that scanning is an important reading skill that requires fast reading. Scanning is reading quickly to find a particular fact or piece of information.

- Go over the steps for successful scanning:
  1. Know the specific information you are looking for: a name, a date, a time, or a key word.
  2. Ignore the words and information that aren't important for your purpose.
  3. Move your eyes quickly across the text until you find the information. Then stop reading.

SKILL FOR SUCCESS: Recognizing Sequence

- Point out that the ability to recognize the sequence of events (the order in which events happen) in a reading passage is an important reading skill.

- Bring in a comic strip with several frames. Use it to illustrate the concept of time order. Have individual students describe what is happening in each frame.

- Introduce the concept of transitions and signal words. Explain that signal words show the relationships between ideas. Writers use signal words to help the reader understand how ideas are related. Go over the list of signal words on page 106. Write an example sentence for each one on the board or have students write the sentences.

EXTRA PRACTICE: Following are some facts about the history of the Olympics, but they are not in the correct order. Have students put them in the correct time order by numbering them from 1 to 7.

_____ Fifteen hundred years later, a Frenchman named Pierre de Coubertin had the idea of organizing a modern Olympics with the goal of encouraging personal excellence and good feeling among countries.

_____ 245 male athletes from fourteen countries competed in nine sports in the 1896 games. No female athletes were present in the 1896 games.

_____ Female athletes competed in the Olympics for the first time in Paris in 1900.

_____ The first recorded Olympic Games took place in Olympia, Greece, in 776 B.C. with one competition, a 200-yard foot race.

_____ Coubertin's dream came true and the first modern Olympics were held in 1896 in Athens, Greece.

_____ Over the years, the ancient Olympic Games grew and other sports such as discus, javelin throw, broad jumping, and wrestling were added.

_____ The games continued to be held every four years at Olympia for over a thousand years until 393 A.D. when the Roman emperor abolished the games because of their pagan influences.

(Correct order: 4, 6, 7, 1, 5, 2, 3)

SKILL FOR SUCCESS: Using Graphic Organizers: Making a Timeline

Remind students that graphic organizers (for example, charts) are helpful tools for organizing information visually. Explain that timelines are another kind of graphic organizer. They show important dates and events.

FYI: Use the official Olympics site to find more information about the Olympics: www.olympic.org

Before You Read

- Read the introduction aloud, or ask for a volunteer to read it to the class.

- Review paraphrasing. Remind students that when they paraphrase, they should express a passage in their own words.

- Go over the interviewer's questions before students read the interview. Make sure they understand what the questions mean.

Reading

This reading is an interview with the renowned sports psychologist Dr. Richard Suinn, who discusses the changing field of sports psychology. He talks about the focus on mental skills that will help athletic performance, such as stress management, visualization, goal-setting, concentration, focus, and relaxation.

After You Read

After students complete Exercise A individually, go over the answers. Ask students to correct the false statements. Invite several students to write their corrected sentences on the board.

SKILL FOR SUCCESS: Summarizing

After students write a summary of the interview, put them in small groups and encourage them to read each other's summaries. Invite several students to read their summaries to the class.

SKILL FOR SUCCESS: Understanding Word Parts: The Prefixes *en-* and *em-*

Explain the meaning of these prefixes. Have students work in pairs to complete the sentences in Exercise D.

Reading Poetry

- Explain the meanings of difficult words before students read the poem:

    buckle down: to start to do something right away

    chuckle: to laugh quietly

    trace: a small amount of something

    scoff: to laugh at a person or idea

    quiddit: *(obsolete)* a quibble, an argument over something unimportant

- Read the poem aloud to the class. Answer any questions students may have about the poem before they read it to themselves.

Discussion

After students discuss the sayings about winning and losing in question 4 on page 119, ask if they have any similar sayings in their culture. Invite students to share them with the class.

Video Activity: Barefoot Marathon

One of the people on the video is Ken Bob Saxton, the founder and president of the Running Barefoot website. Encourage students to look at his website (http://www.runningbarefoot.org) and share some of the information Saxton writes about.

HEALING POWER

Theme: In this unit, students explore topics related to the theme of health.

Readings: The reading in Chapter 1 discusses the use of certain plants to prevent and cure diseases. In Chapter 2, the reading describes the therapeutic powers of music. The reading in Chapter 3 is an article about the role frogs play in the search for new medicines.

Skills for Success: Using Background Knowledge, Taking Notes, Learning Synonyms and Antonyms, Understanding Word Parts: the Suffix -less, Skimming for the Main Idea, Identifying Supporting Information: Quoting Experts, Understanding Anecdotes, Summarizing, Understanding Word Parts: The Prefix -dis, Paraphrasing, Understanding Cause and Effect, Learning Homonyms

Vocabulary:

adaptations	distinguished	predators	supplemental
affectionately	enhances	promoted	therapeutic
beneficial	hooked up to	recovering	toxins
combat	medicinal	remedy	unpalatable
defenses	moderate	stimulate	well-being
disorders	potent	straight	wounds

Points to Ponder

- Read the introduction aloud. Invite students to look at the picture, and ask for a volunteer to describe it.

- If possible, bring in a sample recording of hip-hop music and a song by Frank Sinatra. Find out if any of the students like hip-hop or Sinatra.

Chapter 1: Plant Power (pages 126–132)

Before You Read

- In many countries, plants are used as medicines. Ask students to talk about the types of plants people use for medicine. What illnesses or problems are they used for?

- Bring in samples of the foods discussed in the article: chiles, garlic, ginger, and tea. Ask if the students eat or drink any of them when they feel sick.

Reading

The article describes four plants that are used to prevent and cure diseases: chile peppers, garlic, ginger, and tea.

FYI: This site has pictures and information on the therapeutic benefits of many plants: www.plantcultures.org.uk/plants/ginger_landing.html

SKILL FOR SUCCESS: Taking Notes

- Explain that taking notes while you read is a good way to help you understand and remember what you read. Point out that there are many ways to take notes, and students are going to practice taking "two-column notes."

- Have students look at the setup for two-column notes on page 130. Use the notes on garlic to show how the topic or main idea is written in the left column and supporting information (such as details or examples) is written in the right column.

- Point out that it is not necessary or advisable to write complete sentences.

- Give students a list of common abbreviations in English:

dec or decrease	$ or money, cost, price	etc. or et cetera, and so forth
inc or increase	~ or approximately	b/c, bec or because
& or and	∴ or therefore	b/4 or before
@ or at	# or no. or number	yr or year
/ or per	w/ or with	vs or versus, as opposed to
+ or in addition, and, also	w/o or without	diff or difference
= or equal to	e.g. or for example	info or information
↑ or not equal, is not	ex. or example	impt or important

SKILL FOR SUCCESS: Understanding Word Parts: The Suffix -less

- Explain that the suffix -less is often added to words to mean *without*. Make sure students understand the meanings of *colorless* and *odorless*.

- Write some additional examples: *friendless, meaningless*.

Chapter 2: Music's Surprising Power to Heal (pages 133–141)

Before You Read

After students discuss the questions in Exercise A in pairs, bring the class together and invite individual students to share their responses with their classmates. Generate a list of the kinds of music students use to relax.

SKILL FOR SUCCESS: Skimming for the Main Idea

- Review the steps for skimming an article.

- After students complete the skimming questions, go over the answers with the class.

Reading

The article discusses the ways music can help heal sick people. Doctors and experts in the field of music therapy describe the therapeutic benefits of music, including how music helps to avoid serious complications during illness, enhances patients' well-being, and shortens their hospital stays.

After You Read

After students complete Exercise A individually, go over the answers with the whole class.

SKILL FOR SUCCESS: Identifying Supporting Information: Quoting Experts

- Explain that quotes from experts are often used to support a writer's ideas.

- After students complete the chart with the names, occupations, and quotes of the experts, put them in small groups to discuss the quotes.

SKILL FOR SUCCESS: Understanding Anecdotes

Encourage students to reread the first paragraph of the article. Explain that the story about Ginny is an anecdote.

SKILLS FOR SUCCESS: The Prefix _dis-_

- Explain the meaning of the prefix _dis-_. Write the word _obey_ on the board. Ask students what obey means. (_to follow the instructions, to do what you are told_) Then add the prefix _dis-_ to the word and ask how the meaning changes. (_The prefix_ dis- _changes a word into its opposite._)

- Have students complete Exercise C individually and then compare answers with a partner's answers. Then have them complete a word chart:

Prefix		Word		New word	New meaning
dis	+	honest	=	dishonest	not honest
dis	+	agree	=		
dis	+	respect	=		
dis	+	approve	=		
dis	+	believe	=		
dis	+	like	=		

Chapter 3: Frogs and Human Health (pages 142–150)

Reading

This article discusses the ways frogs can benefit human health. The author explains that frogs have developed unique chemical adaptations that are important in the search for new, more effective medicines. Unfortunately, due to habitat loss, many species of frogs are becoming extinct before scientists get a chance to study them.

SKILL FOR SUCCESS: Understanding Cause and Effect

- Introduce the concept of cause and effect. Read the explanation on page 146 aloud. Be sure to explain the meaning of _cause_ and _effect_. Point out that a cause is a reason. It makes something happen. An effect is a result.

- Go over the list of signal words. Write a sentence on the board using each word.

- After students complete Exercise C on page 147, invite several students to write their answers on the board.

SKILL FOR SUCCESS: Learning Homonyms

- Explain that homonyms are words that are spelled the same or sound the same but have different meanings. Go over the example sentences with the word _treat_. Make sure students understand the two different meanings of _treat_.

- Point out that when a word changes parts of speech, the pronunciation often changes. For example, the adjective _perfect_ is pronounced with the stress on the first syllable, while the verb _perfect_ is pronounced with the second syllable stressed.

- When students have completed Exercise C, ask for volunteers to read each sentence aloud. Correct pronunciation as needed.

Video Activity: Matthew Savage, Jazz Pianist

- Three of Matt Savage's favorite jazz musicians are Dizzy Gillespie, Sonny Rollins, and Thelonious Monk. Bring in some recordings of these musicians for students to listen to.

- Encourage students to research other artists with autism such as:

Hikari Oe (Japan)
Stephen Wiltshire (Britain)
Gilles Trehin (France)
Yeak Ping Lian (Malaysia)
Derek Paravicini (Britian)

UNIT 6 — CRIME

Theme: This unit deals with the theme of crime.

Readings: The reading in Chapter 1 discusses art theft, one of the most frequently committed international crimes. In Chapter 2, the reading is about the developing field of forensics. The reading in Chapter 3 explores the illegal trade of rare and endangered animals.

Skills for Success: Using Graphic Organizers: Charts, Scanning for Information, Learning Two-Word Verbs with *Pull*, Previewing and Predicting, Underlining Important Information, Understanding Word Parts: The Suffix -*ist,* Using Background Knowledge, Summarizing, Understanding Word Parts: The Prefixes *il-* , *ir-*, *im-* and *in-*

Vocabulary:

astute	dreadful	monotonous	ransom
concealed	evidence	obscure	smuggle
confessed	getting away with	on the brink of	tracking down
convicted	guilty	penalties	trafficking
cracking down on	legitimate	poachers	wear and tear
disasters	makes or breaks	pulled off	witnesses

Points to Ponder

- Read the introduction aloud or ask one of the students to volunteer to read it.

- Invite a student to describe the pictures on page 157. Ask another student to read the caption aloud.

Chapter 1: They're Stealing Our Masterpieces (pages 158–165)

Before You Read

Print out some copies of famous paintings that have been stolen and see if students recognize any of them. You can find lists of stolen art and pictures by clicking on the links at this site: www.saztv.com/page28.html

Reading

The article discusses art theft and describes some famous cases of art theft.

FYI: Check out websites about art theft such as www.fbi.gov/hq/cid/arttheft/arttheft.htm.

SKILL FOR SUCCESS: Scanning for Information

Give students a two-minute time limit to complete Exercise C. Then have students compare their answers with a partner's answers.

SKILL FOR SUCCESS: Learning Two-Word Verbs with *Pull*

- Read the explanation of two-word verbs, and go over the examples on page 164. Make sure students understand that the meaning of a two-word verb is different from the meanings of the individual words. Explain that phrasal verbs are made of a verb and a preposition. The combination gives the phrase a special meaning.

- Explain that some phrasal verbs, such as, *pull through,* must have their two parts together, while others, such as, *pull off,* can be separated by one or more words.

- Have students keep a list of the phrasal verbs they learn in their notebooks.

EXTRA PRACTICE:

- Have students work in pairs to brainstorm a list of other phrasal verbs and their definitions.

- Have groups share their lists and definitions.

- Have students make sentences that use each phrasal verb correctly.

Chapter 2: Crime Lab (pages 166–171)

Before You Read

- Introduce the topic of forensics and explain that it is the application of science to solving crimes. Explain that forensic scientists use the tools of science to analyze physical evidence left from a crime.

- Ask students if they know what physical evidence is. Help them understand that fingerprints, hair samples, fibers from fabric, the remains of soil, and blood are all examples of physical evidence. Point out that by using the tools of science, trained forensic-science professionals can analyze these samples to learn more about the person or persons who may have left them behind.

- This article is more challenging. It might be helpful to do some extra preparation before students read. For example, review the target vocabulary words before they read the article. Encourage students to write sentences using the words.

SKILL FOR SUCCESS: Previewing and Predicting

Encourage students to preview the article by looking at the title and headings and then to skim it by reading the first paragraph, the last paragraph, and the first sentence of all the other paragraphs. Also have students look at the photo and read the caption. Make sure they know what a skull is.

SKILL FOR SUCCESS: Underlining Important Information

Read the explanation in the Student Book aloud. Ask if anyone already uses this technique. Point out that like taking notes, underlining is a useful technique for improving comprehension and memory.

Reading

The article is about the field of forensic science and discusses topics including the history of forensics, types of forensic scientists, and how evidence is analyzed.

FYI: This site has a lot of interesting information about forensics. It is designed for teachers and includes definitions, a timeline, and cases: www.courttv.com/ forensics_curriculum.

After You Read

After students complete Exercise B on page 170, have them compare their answers with a partner's answers.

SKILL FOR SUCCESS: Understanding Word Parts: The Suffix *-ist*

- Explain the meaning of the suffix *-ist* using the example *pianist*.
- Point out that there are several suffixes in English that mean "someone who." Explain that, as a teacher, your work is to teach. The suffix *-er* also means "someone who." Other suffixes that mean "someone who" are *-er, -or*, and *-ian*. Help students generate a list of words with these suffixes. Ask questions such as:

  What do you call someone who works with music? What other professionals end in *-ian*?
  What do you call someone who acts on stage? What other professionals end in *-or*?
  What do you call a person who puts out fires? What other professionals end in *-er*?
  What do you call someone whose work is science?

EXTRA PRACTICE: Have students work in pairs to complete a suffix chart like this:

Suffix	Job	Clue
-or		helps sick people
-ian		tells jokes
-ist		works on your teeth
-ist		checks your eyes and vision
-ian		solves math problems
-or		oversees publication of a book, newspaper or magazine
-ist		fills a prescription
-ian		works in politics
-or		Leads an orchestra

Before You Read

Using Background Knowledge

Encourage students to think about what they already know about the illegal sale of rare animals. Read the statements in the chart aloud and ask students to check whether they agree or disagree with each one.

Reading

This article describes crimes that involve trafficking in the sale of rare animals and measures being taken to prevent them.

FYI: These sites have information and links relating to the illegal trade of rare animals:
www.ourplanet.com/imgversn/105/kendall.html
www.panda.org/about_wwf/what_we_do/species/problems/illegal_trade/index.cfm

This article has an interesting twist: The illegal trade in wild animal products over the Internet is driving the world's most endangered species to extinction.
http://news.bbc.co.uk/2/hi/science/nature/4153726.stm

After You Read

After students read the article, invite them to revisit the statements on the chart on page 172. Students should look at the statements they chose before they read to see if they have changed their opinions. Have them record their new responses in the After You Read columns. Ask them to justify their new or continuing opinions based on information in the reading.

SKILL FOR SUCCESS: Understanding Word Parts: The Prefixes il-, ir-, im-, and in-

* Read the explanation of these prefixes and go over the spelling rules.

* After students write their sentences in Exercise D, ask for volunteers to write their sentences on the board.

EXTRA PRACTICE: Explain that English has several prefixes that change a word to its opposite or mean *no* or *not*. Review the prefixes *un-* and *dis-*. Introduce the other prefixes in the following chart.

Prefix	Meaning	Example
dis-	not	disobey
il-, im-, in-, ir-	not	illegal, impractical, inappropriate, irrational
mis-	badly, wrongly	misuse
non-	not	nonsense
un-	not	unable

Take a Survey

Encourage students to bring their completed surveys to class. Have them discuss and compare their results in small groups.

Video Activity: Saving the Elephants

In the video, students heard that baby elephants don't have tusks and often survive the poachers' guns. The rangers bring the orphaned elephants to the Sheldrick Center at the Nairobi National Park to be reared. Encourage students to look at the center's website at http://www.sheldrickwildlifetrust.org. Have them choose an article on the website to read and summarize for the class.

UNIT 7	THE UNIVERSE AND BEYOND

Theme: This unit deals with the theme of space.

Readings: The reading in Chapter 1 describes some of the practical and often unexpected discoveries that come out of research about space travel. In Chapter 2, the reading describes recent research about and travel to the planet Mars. The reading in Chapter 3 is an interview with a physics professor.

Skills for Success: Underlining Important Information, Learning Synonyms and Antonyms, Understanding Word Parts: The Suffix -ize, Skimming for the Main Idea, Identifying Facts and Opinions, Understanding Word Parts: The Suffixes -able and -ible Making Inferences, Understanding Comparisons, Understanding Word Parts: The Suffix -ical

Vocabulary:

anticipated	collaborators	gravity	monitor	shelters
apparent	composition	indefinable	optimum	specialized
arbitrary	device	iron out	precise	spin-offs
automated	distinction	misconception	resistant	was into (something)
boost	durable	missions	rotation	

Points to Ponder

• Have students look at the cartoon. Explain the meaning of the expression *beats me*. (*It is beyond my comprehension; I cannot understand it or work it out.*)

• Invite two volunteers to read the speech bubbles of Alf and Sandy in the cartoon. Explain any other words or expressions students don't know.

• Ask the class to discuss whether or not they think the cartoon is funny.

• Make copies of this quote by Carl Sagan and have students discuss it.

We go about our daily lives understanding almost nothing of the world. We give little thought to the machinery that generates the sunlight that makes life possible, to the gravity that glues us to an Earth that would otherwise send us spinning off into space, or to the atoms of which we are made and on whose stability we fundamentally depend. Except for children (who don't know enough not to ask the important questions), few of us spend much time wondering why nature is the way it is; where the cosmos comes from, or whether it was always here; if time will one day flow backward and effects precede causes; or whether there are ultimate limits to what humans can know.

Before You Read

- Read the introduction to the article aloud.

- Ask students if they know of any practical applications of space research.

SKILL FOR SUCCESS: Underlining Important Information

Explain that the writer of the article used specific examples to support his main ideas. Ask students to underline the main ideas and examples. Point out that the purpose is to complete a chart later in the chapter.

Reading

The article is about the many unexpected practical applications that resulted from the research that went into developing the highly specialized technology for space travel.

FYI: This site gives a sampling of the many other ways that space technology has improved our lives and benefited humankind: www.thespaceplace.com/nasa/spinoffs.html.
The NASA site also provides information on spin-offs that improve our lives in a variety of ways: www.sti.nasa.gov/tto/shuttle.htm.

After You Read

After students complete the chart on page 190, have them share their choices in small groups. Take a class poll to find out the three spin-offs students think are the most valuable.

SKILL FOR SUCCESS: Understanding Word Parts: The Suffix *-ize*

EXTRA PRACTICE:

- Ask students what other words they know that end with the suffix *-ize*. Write them on the board.

- Give students a list of nouns. Have them add the suffix *-ize* to each one to form verbs. They can use dictionaries to check spelling. Have students work alone or in pairs to write original sentences using each of the words as verbs.

author	*final*	*summary*
fantasy	*moral*	*theory*

Before You Read

See how many of the planets students can name in English. Write them on the board as students call out the names.

FYI: Here are some facts about Mars:

- Mars is the fourth planet from the sun and the third smallest, about half the diameter of Earth.

- Mars has a surface area about the same as that of Earth, so there is a lot to explore.

- Mars has varied and fascinating landforms including the largest known volcano in the solar system and a huge canyon system that would stretch across the entire North American continent.

- Unlike Earth, Mars appears to lack active plate tectonics, and there is no evidence of mountain building similar to that we see on our own planet.

- Mars lacks a breathable atmosphere.

- Ice caps are present at both poles.

Reading

This article describes current projects in the exploration of Mars.

SKILL FOR SUCCESS: Identifying Facts and Opinions

Review the difference between facts and opinions. Have students work individually to complete Exercise B on page 197. Then encourage them to compare answers with a partner's answers.

SKILL FOR SUCCESS: Understanding Word Parts: The Suffixes *-able* and *-ible*

- Explain that the suffixes *-able* and *-ible* usually mean that something has that quality or can be done. When these suffixes are added to verbs, they create adjectives (words that describe). Give some examples:

    lovable = worthy of love

    washable = able to be washed

    collectible = worthy of collecting

- Go over the spelling rules:

    If the base word ends with a silent *e*, drop the *e* before adding the suffix *-able*.

    If the base word ends with a consonant + *y*, change the *y* to *i* before adding the suffix *-able*.

    Alternatively, give students this list of words and see if they can figure out the spelling rules:

        remark + able = remark<u>able</u>

        comfort + able = comfort<u>able</u>

        respect + able = respect<u>able</u>

        consider + able = consider<u>able</u>

        predict + able = predict<u>able</u>

        question + able = question<u>able</u>

        favor + able = favor<u>able</u>

        bear + able = bear<u>able</u>

        enjoy + able = enjoy<u>able</u>

        quote + able = quot<u>able</u>

        value + able = valu<u>able</u>

        imagine + able = imagin<u>able</u>

        note + able = not<u>able</u>

        advise + able = advis<u>able</u>

        rely + able = reli<u>able</u>

        vary + able = vari<u>able</u>

        envy + able = envi<u>able</u>

Research a Planet

After students complete their research, have them make posters using the information they found. Display the posters around the room.

Chapter 3: Dancing to the Music of Physics (pages 201–207)

Before You Read

- Read the introduction aloud.

- Explain the meaning of *stereotype* (*a fixed idea that people have about what someone or something is like*).

Reading

In this interview, physicist Steve Huber talks about the connection between art and science.

After You Read

After students complete Exercise A on page 204, ask for a volunteer to read his or her paragraph aloud.

SKILL FOR SUCCESS: Understanding Comparisons

- Give example sentences for the signal words of comparison:

similarly	Tokyo has an efficient subway system. Similarly, London has an efficient subway system.
likewise	Tokyo has an efficient subway system. Likewise, London has an efficient subway system.
like	The climate in Philadelphia is like the climate in Istanbul.
the same	Marsha likes the same kind of music as Isabel.
alike	Louis and Sammy are alike in several ways.
similar to	The population of Vienna is similar to the population of Frankfurt.
the same as	The altitude of Calcutta is the same as the altitude of Copenhagen.
both . . . and	Both China and Korea are in Asia.

- Have students work in pairs to list the three similarities between the arts and science that Dr. Huber discusses in the interview. Then have them share their list with another pair.

Unit 7: Tie It All Together

Video Activity: Rocket Men

Encourage students to work in small groups to make a list of three benefits that could result from private industry's participation in the commercialization of space. Have groups compare their lists.

UNIT 8 — BUSINESS SAVVY

Theme: The articles in this unit are all related to the theme of business and advertising.

Readings: The reading in Chapter 1 discusses the trend of marketing products as "ecofriendly" and "healthy." In Chapter 2, the reading explains some important cultural variables that businessmen and women need to consider when doing business in other countries.

Skills for Success: Skimming for the Main Idea, Learning Idioms, Using Background Knowledge, Previewing and Predicting, Taking Notes, Understanding Contrast, Learning Synonyms and Antonyms, Recognizing Commonly Confused Words

Vocabulary:

abrupt	endeavor	heeding	punctuality
appropriate	exaggerated	minuscule	small talk
blunders	forbidden	offensive	strict
boasts	genuine	poll	subtle
crucial	guidelines	protocol	

Points to Ponder

- Read the introduction aloud or ask one of the students to read it.

- After students discuss the questions, bring the whole class together and make a list of the ways companies do business and how they have changed in the last ten years.

Chapter 1: Nothing but the Truth (pages 214–221)

Before You Read

- Bring in some magazines with ads for products that claim to be good for the environment or good for your health. Distribute the magazines and have students look through them and find the ads.

- Make sure students understand the meanings of *ecofriendly* (*describes a product that has been designed to do the least possible damage to the environment*) and *all-natural* (*containing no artificial ingredients*).

Reading

This article explains the trend of manufacturers and advertisers to market products as "ecofriendly" and "healthy, all-natural."

FYI: Green Seal's website has lots of information related to the theme of this article: www.greenseal.org.

SKILL FOR SUCCESS: Learning Idioms

After students complete the exercise you may want to give them these definitions:

1. jumped on the bandwagon: became involved in a successful activity to get the advantages of it yourself

2. go to these lengths: to try very hard to achieve something

3. laughed all the way to the bank: rejoiced in a financial gain from something that had either been derided or thought worthless

4. crack down: start treating people more strictly to try to stop them from doing things they should not do (usually said of someone in authority, such as, police or government)

Analyzing Ads

EXTRA PRACTICE:

- Invite students to evaluate television ads by keeping a log of the ad that they watch. Have them figure out how many minutes per hour are used for advertising. Tell them to identify their five favorite ads and the five they dislike the most. Encourage them to bring their logs to class and explain why they liked or disliked each of the ads.

- Have students work in groups to create a thirty-second television ad. Have each group think of a real or imaginary product and create a slogan for it. An example might be "Super Snax" and the slogan could be "Super Snax for Super Energy." Encourage students to write a short script for their ad. Have each group perform its ad for the class.

Choose a Title

EXTRA PRACTICE: Have students work in pairs to choose a product that is advertised in several different media, such as television, magazines, and online. Instruct them to analyze an example of each type of ad. Ask pairs to rate the effectiveness of each ad on a scale of 1 to 4.

Chapter 2: Do's and Taboos (pages 222–234)

Before You Read

- Introduce the concept of cultural variables using greetings as an example. Have students look at the picture on page 224 and invite a student to read the caption. Then have the students say or demonstrate several ways they greet people they know on the street. Have them give examples of friends, older people, casual acquaintances, family members, business associates, and so on. Discuss the differences.

- Generate a definition of *culture*. Culture may be defined as the ideas, beliefs, and customs that are shared and accepted by people in a society.

- This is a longer and more challenging article. It will be helpful to have students do some additional prereading activities. Invite a student to read the callouts aloud. Discuss the kind of information they think will be discussed in each section.

- Encourage students to skim this article by reading the first few paragraphs (including paragraph 6), the last paragraph, and the first sentence of all the other paragraphs.

Reading

The article describes cultural variables that affect the way business is conducted.
There is a lot of information on the Internet about doing business in other countries. Here is an interesting website: www.cyborlink.com.

EXTRA PRACTICE: Have students read the following paragraph that describes the differences between two types of learners. Tell them to underline the signal words and complete the chart.

Psychologists have observed that people learn in different ways, absorbing information through different senses. Most people can be classified as either visual learners or auditory learners. Visual learners learn most efficiently with their eyes. They take in information by observing visual cues or by reading information. Auditory learners, on the other hand, learn with their ears. They understand information best by listening to oral clues and hearing information. For example, these two types of learners would use different processes in learning a foreign language. Visual learners learn a new language most effectively by reading books, newspapers, or magazines. They benefit from looking at diagrams, charts, and pictures and reading written directions. In contrast, auditory learners benefit from listening to lectures and CDs, watching movies or television, or having a conversation in the new language. They respond best to precise oral directions and explanations. Of course, most learners use both visual and auditory methods. Researchers report, though, that most of us are likely to use one sense more effectively than the others.

	How They Take in Information	How They Learn a New Language
Visual Learners		
Auditory Learners		

Unit 8: Tie It All Together

Video Activity: Kids and Food

Today many restaurants feature a special "kid's menu" with special dishes for children. Have students work in pairs to make a kid's menu for a restaurant in their country. Tell them to think of at least four healthy dishes that children might like to eat. Also include some healthy drinks and desserts for children. Display the menus around the room.

UNIT TESTS AND ANSWER KEY

Read the article.

A Valuable Alternative

According to an old saying, "To understand another man, you need to walk a mile in his shoes." It is certainly true that it isn't always easy to understand other people's points of view, let alone embrace them. Sometimes, it may require looking at issues from a different perspective. Too often, we assume that our own opinions are based on truth and that those who disagree with us are simply wrong. This can be especially true when it comes to events in the news.

Robin Koerner, who is British, and Will Kern, an American, had a vision of starting a website to promote an understanding of international perspectives. In 2005, they founded the website www.watchingamerica.com. The website, subtitled "Discover What the World Thinks about the U.S.," is composed of English translations of news articles from around the world. The aim of the web site is to broaden the perspective of American readers by allowing them to see how the rest of the world views U.S. foreign policy and other government programs. For example, visitors to www.watchingamerica.com can read about how Colombian, German, Egyptian, Nigerian, or Chinese journalists report on news events related to American policy. The result is that readers are exposed to a variety of voices and multiple opinions, many of which are not always reflected in American coverage of the news. Some of the articles are critical of the U.S. government, while others are more favorable or simply neutral. In addition to foreign policy, other U.S. programs such as NASA, the space program, and economic issues are covered. The website is free to users, but it does have some advertising.

Translations of the articles are done through computer software. Most are then revised by bilingual volunteers. Each article is labeled according to whether it is a "machine" translation or whether is has been edited. All the translated articles have links to the original news source. There are also articles from international journals published in English.

In interviews with American media posted on the website, cofounder Robin Koern discusses why this website is needed in today's world, and he explains that international cooperation must be based on mutual understanding. He quotes British writer John Stuart Mills: "He who knows only his own side of the case knows little of that." Some readers might be offended by some of the views presented on the website, but it is an educational experience for them to discover how others perceive news events. People who depend on reading just one newspaper or watching one TV news station might not realize how limited their information and perspectives are. For people interested in understanding a wide range of voices and developing an international awareness, www.watchingamerica.com provides a valuable alternative.

Part 1 *(13 points)*

A. *Read these statements. If a statement is true, write* **T** *on the line. If it is false, write* **F.**

_____ **1.** Robin Koerner and Will Kern founded the website www.watchingamerica.com.

_____ **2.** Readers of the website are exposed to a variety of voices and opinions that are not always reflected in American newspapers.

_____ **3.** Bilingual volunteers revise and edit all the articles.

_____ **4.** The aim of the website is to teach the rest of the world about the American point of view.

_____ **5.** Readers can tell whether an article has been machine translated or edited.

_____ **6.** Translations of the articles are done through computer software.

_____ **7.** Users must pay a fee to read the articles on the website.

B. *Decide if each statement is a fact or an opinion. Check the correct box.*

Statement	Fact	Opinion
1. Too often, we assume that our own opinions are based on truth and that those who disagree with us are simply wrong.		
2. The website is free to users.		
3. www.watchingamerica.com was founded in 2005.		
4. "He who knows only his own side of the case knows little of that."		
5. All the translated articles have links to the original news source.		
6. For people interested in understanding a wide range of voices and developing an international awareness, www.watchingamerica.com provides a valuable alternative.		

Part 2 *(12 points)*

A. *Choose the best definition for the underlined word in each sentence.*

1. It is certainly true that it isn't always easy to understand other people's points of view, let alone embrace them.

   a. to reject the opinions of others

   b. to eagerly accept ideas and opinions

   c. to try to remember certain ideas

2. The result is that readers are exposed to a variety of voices and multiple opinions.

   a. many

   b. negative

   c. unusual

3. Robin Koerner, who is British, and Will Kern, an American, had a <u>vision</u> of starting a website to promote an understanding of international perspectives.

    a. an investment

    b. a question

    c. a dream

B. *Match each word with its synonym.*

_____ **1.** perspective	a. believe
_____ **2.** valuable	b. understanding
_____ **3.** assume	c. viewpoint
_____ **4.** critical	d. rely
_____ **5.** awareness	e. worthwhile
_____ **6.** depend	f. unfavorable

C. *Circle the correct word form to complete each sentence.*

1. The website is (educate, educator, educational) and informative.

2. He made an interesting (suggest, suggestion, suggestive) at the meeting.

3. Please (respond, response, responsive) as soon as you get my e-mail.

UNIT **2** TEST

Read the article.

Learning about Happiness

How would you like to take a college course that teaches you how to be a happy person? That's what thousands of students around the United States are doing. In the last few years, happiness classes have cropped up at over a hundred colleges around the United States. In fact, the most popular course at Harvard University this semester teaches happiness. The course is called Positive Psychology, and it is based on scientific research. Twice a week, 885 Harvard students crowd into a lecture hall to learn about happiness from the brilliant thirty-five-year-old teacher, Tal D. Ben-Shahar.

The Harvard course is based on the new area of psychology called *positive psychology*. Simply put, positive psychology is the scientific study of human happiness. Positive psychology focuses on what makes people feel good rather than what causes them to feel bad. Until recently, the prevailing focus in the field of psychology has been on mental illness rather than mental wellness. Psychologists asked questions such as why do people get depressed, irritable, or anxious? What causes mental illness? Now some psychologists are examining what makes people happy rather than what makes them sad. Martin Seligman, the illustrious psychologist and professor at the University of Pennsylvania, is the father of positive psychology. Seligman, a former president of the American Psychological Association, first introduced the world to positive psychology in 1998. Simply put, the overall goal of positive psychology is to enhance people's experiences of love, work, and play. One way to achieve this goal is to teach people how to incorporate personal qualities such as humor, originality, and generosity into their interactions with others to achieve happiness. Seligman began offering a course on happiness at the University of Pennsylvania in 2003. He thinks the enthusiasm of his students reflects the appeal of the positive psychology movement in general.

So what does make us happy? Research suggests that once our basic needs are met, factors such as money, education, high intelligence, sunny weather, or even youth have only a modest effect on happiness. What researchers are discovering is that things such as friends and strong family connections directly affect how happy you are with your life. According to Seligman and other positive psychologists, there are certain personal qualities, or strengths, that directly affect happiness. For example, qualities such as curiosity, optimism, courage, humor, kindness, and generosity are very important in leading a happy life. Seligman encourages people to build on the qualities they already possess. For example, if you are already a generous person by nature, then you should try to practice being generous with friends, coworkers, and even strangers on a daily basis. The more generous you are to others, the more meaning you will have in your life and the happier you'll be.

Seligman firmly believes that everyone has the ability to be happy. You just have to put some work into it. Seligman should know, because he is actually a self-proclaimed pessimist and has been very open about his own depressive tendencies. He believes optimism is a quality that can be developed. Seligman argues that it doesn't matter how naturally optimistic or pessimistic you are. People can learn to expand upon their own ability to feel good and develop qualities that lead to happiness. In other words, anyone can lead a happy, if not happier, life.

In his 2002 book *Authentic Happiness*, Seligman describes what he believes are the three areas of life that are the keys to happiness:

The Pleasant Life. This means having as much pleasure and positive emotion as possible—basically, enjoying the things that make you smile. For example, your favorite food, animal, or even article of clothing are all things that would help to put a smile on your face.

The Engaged Life. This has to do with becoming really involved with the people in your life and the activities you pursue. Your family, friends, work, and hobbies are all examples of things you can be engaged with.

The Meaningful Life. Achieving meaning in your life requires going beyond your own pleasures and using your personal strengths in the service of something more important than yourself. Helping others through volunteering can help you to realize that there is something bigger and more important than yourself. So can religion and politics.

Almost every aspect of positive psychology has to do with interacting with other people. In other words, if you have good relationships with the people in your life, work hard to help those around you, and try to interact positively with as many people as possible, then you are more likely to lead a happier life than someone who has little to do with other people. It seems like a no-brainer, but the next time you find yourself feeling sad or depressed, think about calling up some friends to tell them how much they mean to you. You'll be surprised at how much happier you'll feel. And happiness is contagious. Your friends will probably feel happier too!

Part 1 *(12 points)*

A. *Circle the correct answer.*

1. According to Seligman, which quality is NOT a personal strength that directly affects happiness?

   a. curiosity

   b. optimism

   c. intelligence

2. What is positive psychology mainly concerned with?

   a. what makes people feel good

   b. what causes people to feel bad

   c. how mental illness affects society

3. What does Seligman encourage people to do?

   a. spend a lot of time studying

   b. build on the strengths they already possess

   c. become less involved in their work and hobbies

B. *Check the statements you can infer based on the information in the article.*

_____ 1. Education has a stronger effect on happiness then money.

_____ 2. Generosity is the most important quality to develop if you want to be happy.

_____ 3. Even pessimistic people can learn to be happier.

_____ 4. In general, women are happier than men.

_____ 5. According to positive psychologists, if you are already a curious person by nature, then you should try to build on that strength.

_____ **6.** People who spend a lot of time socializing are often happier than people who spend most of their time alone.

_____ **7.** Psychologists are no longer concerned with the causes of mental illness.

_____ **8.** Eating your favorite candy will help you achieve a meaningful life.

_____ **9.** Getting a pay raise probably won't have a big impact on your happiness.

Part 2 *(12 points)*

A. *Choose the best definition or synonym for the underlined word in each sentence.*

1. Until recently, the <u>prevailing</u> focus in the field of psychology has been on mental illness rather than mental wellness.

   a. uncommonly used

   b. most common at a particular time

   c. difficult to understand

2. Why do people get depressed, <u>irritable</u>, or anxious?

   a. annoyed

   b. thirsty

   c. hopeful

3. Martin Seligman, the <u>illustrious</u> psychologist and professor at the University of Pennsylvania, is the father of positive psychology.

   a. young and untraditional

   b. famous and well-respected

   c. intelligent but unknown

4. It seems like a <u>no-brainer</u>, but the next time you find yourself feeling sad or depressed, think about calling up some friends to tell them how much they mean to you.

   a. easy to understand and do

   b. the most difficult

   c. very confusing

5. Research suggests that once our basic needs are met, factors such as money, education, high intelligence, sunny weather, or even youth have only a <u>modest</u> effect on happiness.

   a. not large

   b. very large

   c. unpredictable

6. And happiness is <u>contagious</u>. Your friends will probably feel happier too!

   a. traditional and ordinary

   b. difficult to achieve

   c. transmitted from one person to another

7. The teacher is the <u>brilliant</u> thrity-five-year-old Tal D. Ben-Shahar.

    a. very pleasant

    b. extremely bright and capable

    c. mediocre

B. *Complete each sentence with the correct word from the list.*

mistrust	misbehave	misguided
miscounted	misunderstood	

1. I hope the children don't _____ while I'm gone.

2. I thought I had four dollars in my wallet, but I only have three. I must have

    _____ .

3. You shouldn't marry someone if you _____ him or her.

4. I am completely lost. I must have _____ the directions you gave me.

5. She made a _____ attempt to resolve the problem.

UNIT 3 **TEST**

Read the article.

Stay-at-Home Dads

When Jason and Melinda Wolf had their first child five years ago, the couple made an important decision. They decided that Jason would quit his job and stay home to take care of the baby. Since Melinda made more money at her job as a dentist than Jason did, it made more sense for Melinda to continue working. It was supposed to be a temporary arrangement. They would hire a full-time babysitter when the baby was six months old and Jason would go back to his job as an electrical engineer. But things changed. Today, five years and three children later, Jason is still home. He loved his role as a stay-at-home father so much that he decided not to go back to working outside the home. Jason is not alone in his role. And he thoroughly enjoys it. According to Jason, "If you are up for the challenges, stay-at-home parenting can be a wonderful experience for fathers and for the whole family."

Like other two-career couples, the Wolfs decided that it didn't really make sense for both of them to keep working after they had children. They figured out the cost of maintaining two incomes. "After we deducted the cost of child care, higher income taxes and car insurance, work clothes, and lunches, we realized that if both of us worked, we made only a few thousand dollars more," Jason says.

Traditionally the mother has been the parent to take on the responsibility of raising the children and taking care of the home. Most fathers accepted the conventional family role of wage earner and financial provider. But the number of stay-at-home dads is growing each year. The latest statistics show 143,000 fathers who stay home primarily to take care of their children. This is an increase of nearly 50 percent since 1999. These men, who are all married fathers with children under fifteen years old, have stayed out of the labor force for more than one year to care for the family while their wives work outside the home.

Some men decide to become stay-at-home dads because their wives earn higher salaries than they do. Others want to spend more time with their children. Most admit that raising children isn't easy. Jason says, "It is the hardest job in the world, but it's also the most rewarding. I wouldn't give it up for anything."

Although the number of stay-at-home dads continues to grow, these men still face many challenges. According to Jason Wolf and most other stay-at-home fathers, the biggest challenge they face is the sense of isolation. Stay-at-home dads often feel like outsiders in a world of mothers and children. "When I'm at the park with my kids, the other mothers don't include me in their conversations. I get the feeling they think I'm a loser who can't find a job. If someone does talk to me, it's usually just to ask a question like, 'Are you baby-sitting today?'"

To overcome his sense of isolation, Curtis Cooper, a stay-at-home dad in St. Paul, Minnesota, started the DAD-to-DAD organization in January 1995. The organization began as a way for dads to get together and share information while their children played. The idea caught on, and today there are thirty DAD-to-DAD groups around the country where dads can connect with each other in their local areas.

Even today there still seems to be a social stigma attached to being a full-time care-giving father. As we progress into the new millennium, it remains more culturally acceptable for a mother to stay home than it is for a father. "The challenge facing SAHDs comes from society's view of what role the man should and should not play in the family," says Curtis Cooper. "Many men and women still believe that it is the woman's place to stay home and raise the children." Jason Wolf admits that even his own parents tried to dissuade him when he announced that he was quitting his job in order to stay home with the baby. His friends were stunned as well when he made the decision to be a stay-at-home dad. He says, "It's absurd to think that fathers can't be as conscientious, nurturing, and effective as mothers when it comes to raising children."

In the past, most resources for parents were aimed at mothers. But today, dads can get advice as well, especially from the Internet. For example, www.Slowlane.com is an excellent online reference, resource, and network for stay-at-home fathers and their families. The www.Slowlane.com site gives dads a collection of articles written by, for, and about stay-at-home fathers. It has links to websites for local DAD-to-DAD chapters. An on-line magazine called www.Fathermag.com is also a helpful resource. There are several new books for fathers who are raising their children, too. One of the most popular is called *The Stay-at-Home Dad Handbook*. This excellent book offers valuable suggestions and practical advice for mastering the stay-at-home dad's roles.

As the number of stay-at-home dads continues to grow, there is more and more support available for them. There is even an annual convention for stay-at-home fathers. Called the At-Home Dads Convention, it attracts fathers from around the country who want to network, share experiences, and participate in workshops with their peers. Some of the most popular workshops include Kids, Nutrition, and Behavior; Keeping Track of Your Kids on the Internet; Informational Resources for At-Home Dads; Investing for the Future; and Child Safety.

Although the change from working outside the home to staying home to raise the children has its challenges, the men who have done it believe that the advantages outweigh the sacrifices. For the time being, the number of SAHDs may be small, but they are making a difference. You may even see some men proudly wearing T-shirts that declare "Men Who Change Diapers Change the World," and I believe they do.

Part 1 *(11 points)*

A. *Read these statements. If a statement is true, write* **T** *on the line. If it is false, write* **F.**

_____ **1.** The number of stay-at-home dads is decreasing year by year.

_____ **2.** Jason Wolf enjoys his role as a care-giving father.

_____ **3.** There are fewer books about parenting for mothers than for fathers.

_____ **4.** It is still more culturally acceptable for a mother to stay home than it is for a father.

_____ **5.** Local DAD-to-DAD groups offer stay-at-home fathers a way to interact with their peers.

_____ **6.** Most stay-at-home dads think their job is easy.

_____ **7.** The *Stay-at-Home Dad Handbook* offers readers practical advice.

B. *Circle the correct answer.*

1. What is the tone of the article?

    a. humorous

    b. admiring

    c. disapproving

2. Which conclusion can you infer from the article?

   a. It often takes a long time for cultural attitudes to change.

   b. Stay-at-home fathers make better parents than do stay-at-home mothers.

   c. Most stay-at-home fathers have a large network of support.

3. Where would a stay-at-home father be most likely to find helpful resources?

   a. in a bookstore

   b. at the library

   c. on the Internet

4. Many stay-at-home fathers say that the biggest challenge they face is _____.

   a. their sense of isolation

   b. the loss of their income

   c. the lack of resources

Part 2 *(14 points)*

A. *Read each pair of words. Write an **S** if they are synonyms. Write an **A** if they are antonyms.*

1. conventional	traditional	_____
2. peers	colleagues	_____
3. strive	try hard	_____
4. absurd	reasonable	_____
5. conscientious	careless	_____
6. stunned	shocked	_____
7. dissuade	encourage	_____

B. *Circle the correct word to complete each sentence.*

1. Hurry up. (It's / Its) already noon. I don't want to be late.

2. I would rather work outside the home (than / then) at home.

3. My doctor told me that I needed to (loose / lose) weight.

4. The workshop about child safety is in the conference room. You should be (there / their) at 2:00 P.M.

5. This car is (to / too) expensive. I can't afford to buy it.

6. At night, the house is dark and (quiet / quite).

7. The children are playing with (their / they're) friends.

Read the article.

"Babe," the First Lady of Golf

Mildred Ella Didrikson was born June 26, 1914, in Port Arthur, Texas, the child of Norwegian immigrants. As a child, Didrikson played baseball and got the nickname "Babe" because people thought she hit as well as the famous baseball player Babe Ruth. Known throughout her life as "Babe," she is often called the First Lady of Golf. Many people consider her to be one of the greatest athletes in sports history. Babe became famous for her ability as a golfer, but she was an amazing athlete and competitor in many other sports as well. This may sound like Hollywood fiction, but it is a true story.

Even as a child, Babe was very competitive, and it was obvious that she had great athletic potential. Everyone knew that Babe could run faster, jump higher, throw farther, and play any game better than anyone she played against. As a teenager, she played professional basketball. Then she decided to try track and field, and she won two gold medals and a silver medal at the 1932 summer Olympic Games in Los Angeles, California. Between 1930 and 1932, she held American, Olympic, and world records in five different track and field sports. Meanwhile, Babe took up other sports, including football, boxing, and baseball. She excelled in all of them. Because Babe was so good at so many sports, sports writer Grantland Rice called her the "athlete phenomenon of our time."

After the 1932 Olympics Babe turned to golf, and in 1934 she won her first tournament. She fell in love with the game of golf and from then on devoted herself to it. Combining her natural talent with hard work, she would hit over a thousand balls a day, eight to ten hours a day. In 1938, Babe married former professional wrestler George Zaharias, who became her biggest fan and supporter. She won seventeen straight amateur tournaments, and in 1947 she became the first American to win the prestigious British Women's Amateur Championship. All in all, Babe won eighty-two golf tournaments in her twenty-year career. In 1949 she became one of the founding members of the Ladies' Professional Golf Association. Babe was a high-profile player, the first female golf celebrity in the United States and the leading player of the 1940s and early 1950s. She loved playing for an audience, and spectators clapped and cheered every time she won another tournament.

In the spring of 1953, Babe was diagnosed with cancer and had surgery. Some people thought that her athletic career was over, but Babe played in a golf tournament only fourteen weeks after the surgery. The next year she won five tournaments, including the U.S. Women's Open. Then in 1955, her doctors discovered that the cancer had returned. Babe was in great pain, but she continued to play her favorite game. Babe's courage during her illness served as an inspiration for many Americans. She died in Galveston on September 27, 1956.

Before her death in 1956, Babe had won eighty-two amateur and professional titles. On six occasions, the Associated Press named her the Female Athlete of the Year. In an Associated Press poll in 1950, Babe was voted Woman Athlete of the First Half of the Twentieth Century. Then in 1999, she was voted Woman Athlete of the Twentieth Century. That same year, *Sports Illustrated* magazine also named her the Female Athlete of the Century. Her autobiography, called *This Life I've Led*, was published in 1955.

In an article for *Sports Illustrated*, the sportswriter Paul Gallico wrote a tribute to Babe after her death. He said, "Much has been made of Babe Didrikson's natural aptitude for sports, as well as her competitive spirit and indomitable will to win. But not enough has been said about the patience and strength of character expressed in her willingness to practice endlessly and her recognition that she could reach the top and stay there only by incessant hard work." It is no surprise that Babe remains a sports legend and role model to many aspiring athletes.

Part 1 *(13 points)*

A. *Read these statements. If a statement is true, write* **T** *on the line. If it is false, write* **F***.*

_____ **1.** Babe was an amazing athlete and competitor in a variety of sports.

_____ **2.** In the 1932 Olympics, Babe won several medals for golf.

_____ **3.** Few people believe that Babe was one of the greatest athletes in all of sports history.

_____ **4.** Babe wrote a book about her life called *This Life I've Led.*

_____ **5.** Sportswriter Paul Gallico admired Babe.

_____ **6.** Babe's courage during her illness inspired many people.

B. *Number these events so that they are in the order in which they happened in Babe's life.*

_____ Won the British Women's Amateur Championship

_____ Died in 1956

_____ Won her first golf tournament

_____ Married George Zaharias

_____ Born in Port Arthur, Texas

_____ Won two gold medals and a silver medal at the 1932 Olympics

_____ Diagnosed with cancer

Part 2 *(9 points)*

A. *Choose the best definition or synonym for the underlined word in each sentence.*

1. Even as a child, Babe was very competitive, and it was obvious that she had great athletic potential.

a. difficulty

b. promise

c. confidence

2. Babe was a high-profile player, the first female golf celebrity in the United States and the leading player of the 1940s and early 1950s.

a. attracting a lot of attention from people

b. disappointing many people

c. relatively unknown

3. She loved playing for an audience, and spectators clapped and <u>cheered</u> every time she won another tournament.

    a. began to cry

    b. jumped up and down

    c. gave loud shouts of approval

B. *Read each pair of words. Write an* **S** *if they are synonyms. Write an* **A** *if they are antonyms.*

1. triumph	failure	_____
2. spectators	audience	_____
3. perseverance	determination	_____

C. *Add the suffix –ance or –ence to each word to make a noun.*

1. exist _____

2. perform _____

3. accept _____

UNIT **5**   **TEST**

Read the article.

Scents Make Sense

Do you ever feel tired or stressed after a long day at work or school? Or do you ever feel a bit blue or depressed during the long winter months? Then aromatherapy may be just the thing for you. Aromatherapy is the practice of using the aromatic oils from plants as a form of therapy for improving your physical health and emotional well-being. The oils, called essential oils, used in aromatherapy are found in different parts of the plant, such as the flowers, leaves, bark, or in the skin of fruit. For example, in roses and jasmine, the essential oils are found in the flowers, in basil it is in the leaves, and in sandalwood it is in the wood.

There are several ways to extract the essential oils from a plant. The two most common methods are called "steam distillation" and "cold pressing." In steam distillation, the flowers or leaves of the plant are heated by steam from boiling water. The vapors that result are then separated into scented water and essential oils. Cold pressing is used to extract the essential oils from the skin of citrus fruits, such as oranges and lemons. The skin is separated from the fruit and then chopped and pressed. The result is a watery mixture of essential oil and water, which eventually separates.

Aromatherapy as a method of natural healing is not new. In fact, the practice dates back thousands of years. The ancient Greeks, Romans, Chinese, Indians, Persians, and Egyptians all appreciated the therapeutic benefits of aromatherapy. The Chinese and the Egyptians were probably the first to understand the wonderful effects of aromatherapy. The Chinese used aromatic plants by burning them to promote harmony and balance. The Egyptians invented a simple machine to extract oil from cedar wood. The Greeks also recognized the medicinal and aromatic benefits of plants. In fact, the Greek doctor Hippocrates, often called the father of medicine, used aromatherapy baths and scented massage. In 400 B.C., Hippocrates wrote, "The way to health is to have an aromatic bath and scented massage every day."

Over the years interest in aromatherapy seemed to die out. Then, in the 1920s, a chance incident sparked a renewed interest in the healing powers of essential oils. René Gattefosse was a French chemist who worked in his family's perfume business. One day, while he was working in his laboratory, he burned his hand in an explosion. He quickly put his hand into a bowl of lavender oil. To his amazement, the burn on his hand healed very quickly, without infection or scarring. Fascinated by the benefits of lavender oil, Gattefosse began to investigate the effects of other essential oils for healing. His research led him to write a book called *Aromatherapies*. The book was well received by other scientists who went on to do their own research.

Oils with different fragrances are used by aromatherapists to increase energy, reduce stress, and relax muscle aches, along with other benefits. For example, orange and rose oils are both considered relaxing, and aromatherapy experts say that the smell of these oils can reduce anxiety or aid in sleeping. Lemon and peppermint are extremely refreshing and stimulating, and they are used to help digestion and combat fatigue. Lavender oil has the most wonderful smell. Its most common use is in treating headaches and insomnia and in reducing stress. It is also used as a remedy for coughs and colds.

There are several ways to enjoy the benefits of aromatherapy. The fragrant oils can be applied directly on the skin through a lotion or rubbed in with a massage. Another method is to take a bath with drops of the oil mixed with hot water. For less intense aromatherapy, candles scented with essential oils can be burned to create a fragrant smell in the air. Of course, it is important to follow guidelines for specific amounts and forms of application. Keep in mind that some of the oils are very potent and must be diluted before use.

Part 1 *(12 points)*

Circle the correct answer.

1. Which paragraph gives a definition of aromatherapy?

   a. paragraph 1

   b. paragraph 2

   c. paragraph 3

2. Which paragraph discusses aromatherapy in ancient times?

   a. paragraph 3

   b. paragraph 4

   c. paragraph 5

3. Which procedure is NOT a method of extracting the essential oils from a plant?

   a. cold pressing

   b. scented massages

   c. steam distillation

4. According to the article, what is peppermint used for?

   a. to stimulate digestion and combat fatigue

   b. to treat headaches and insomnia

   c. to fight coughs and colds

5. Where is the essential oil in basil found?

   a. in the flowers

   b. in the leaves

   c. in the stem

6. René Gattefosse discovered the healing power of lavender _____ .

   a. by experimentation

   b. by reading books

   c. by accident

7. Which of the following is a less intense form of aromatherapy?

   a. burning a candle scented with essential oils

   b. having a massage with essential oils

   c. taking a bath with a few drops of an essential oil

8. _____ of the oils should be diluted before you use them.

    a. Some

    b. All

    c. None

9. Which paragraph describes the ways to enjoy aromatherapy?

    a. paragraph 2

    b. paragraph 4

    c. paragraph 6

10. Which statement is NOT an inference you can make based on the article?

    a. There are more than two ways to extract oils from plants.

    b. Lavender oil helps prevent scarring.

    c. Lemon oil is more affective than peppermint oil for stimulating digestion.

11. Which statement is an opinion of the author of the article?

    a. René Gattefosse wrote a book called *Aromatherapies*.

    b. Lavender oil has the most wonderful smell.

    c. The Egyptians invented a simple machine to extract oil from cedar wood.

12. The tone of the article is _____ .

    a. critical

    b. humorous

    c. favorable

Part 2 *(10 points)*

A. *Read each pair of words. Write an **S** if they are synonyms. Write an **A** if they are antonyms.*

1. potent	weak	_____
2. medicinal	therapeutic	_____
3. cure	remedy	_____
4. well-being	unhappiness	_____
5. stimulate	promote	_____
6. beneficial	harmful	_____
7. aromatic	odorless	_____

B. *Write the part of speech above each underlined word.*

1. a. Lemon and peppermint are used to <u>combat</u> fatigue.

    b. There was a long <u>combat</u> between the two sides.

2. a. We like to buy fresh <u>produce</u> in the summer.

    b. Many plants <u>produce</u> fragrant oils.

3. a. Aromatherapy can <u>benefit</u> people who suffer from stress.

    b. There are many <u>benefits</u> of aromatherapy.

Read the article.

The Scream and *Madonna* Recovered

Although art theft is on the rise, art lovers around the world recently had a reason to celebrate. Two of the world's most famous paintings, *The Scream* and *Madonna* by artist Edvard Munch, which had been missing for over two years, were recently recovered. *The Scream*, painted in 1893, is one of the world's most recognizable paintings. Art experts estimated its value at over $70 million.

The Oslo police found the paintings during an organized raid. Although they won't say where the paintings were found, police think they were in Norway all along. No details were given about how police were led to the location where the paintings were hidden.

"We are 100 percent certain they are the originals. The damage was much less than feared," police said. Iver Stensrud was the head of the police investigation. At a news conference he reported that the condition of the paintings was better than expected. The paintings were examined by museum experts who said they suffered some wear and tear. *The Scream* had minor damage in one corner, and *Madonna* had a small rip in its canvas. They also had some scratches, but museum experts said both could be repaired.

In August 2004, the two masterpieces were stolen in broad daylight from the Munch Museum in Oslo, Norway. In one of the most publicized art thefts in history, two thieves wearing ski masks walked into the museum and grabbed the paintings right off the wall as stunned museum visitors and employees watched helplessly. One of the thieves even threatened a staff member with a gun before he and his partner escaped into a waiting car.

Soon after the theft, the getaway car was recovered and police discovered some evidence. They found parts of the frames of the paintings. During the years the paintings were missing, many people feared that the irreplaceable masterpieces had been lost forever. Norwegian news media speculated about the fate of the treasured paintings. Some experts worried that the paintings had been destroyed to get rid of the evidence. Others believed that they had been sold to a wealthy private collector or damaged in their hiding place.

The paintings were recovered after an intense international police operation and an offer of a $300,000 reward for information about the robbery by the city of Oslo. In May 2006, police arrested three men connected to the robbery. They were sentenced to up to eight years in prison for their roles in the theft. Bjoern Hoen was convicted of planning the robbery and sentenced to seven years in jail. Petter Tharaldsen got eight years after he confessed to driving the getaway car. And Petter Rosenvinge was sentenced to four years for supplying the vehicle. Unfortunately, police still have not caught the masked gunmen who actually pulled off the heist. Maybe they got away with it after all.

After the theft of the Munch paintings, the museum closed for nine months to complete a $6.4 million security upgrade. Today, valuable paintings are behind bulletproof glass, and all visitors must go through metal detectors and baggage scanners to enter.

Part 1 *(13 points)*

A. *Scan the article for the answer to each question.*

1. How much did the city of Oslo offer as a reward for information about the robbery?

_____

2. Who drove the getaway car? _____

3. When were the paintings stolen? _____

4. How much did the security upgrade of the museum cost? _____

5. Who was the head of the police investigation? _____

6. Which painting had a small rip in its canvas? _____

B. *Read these statements. If a statement is true, write* **T** *on the line. If it is false, write* **F.**

_____ **1.** *The Scream* and *Madonna* were painted by artist Edvard Munch.

_____ **2.** The thieves led the police to the location where the paintings were hidden.

_____ **3.** Both paintings were greatly damaged.

_____ **4.** One of the thieves threatened a staff member with a gun.

_____ **5.** *The Scream* is a relatively obscure painting.

_____ **6.** The masked gunmen who actually stole the paintings are in jail.

_____ **7.** *The Scream* and *Madonna* are now protected by bulletproof glass.

Part 2 *(12 points)*

A. *Choose the best synonym or definition for the underlined word or phrase in each sentence.*

1. Petter Tharaldsen got eight years after he <u>confessed</u> to driving the getaway car.

   a. denied

   b. admitted

   c. questioned

2. The paintings were examined by museum experts who said they suffered some <u>wear and tear</u>.

   a. damage caused over a period of time

   b. great improvements

   c. major damage

3. Unfortunately, police still have not caught the masked gunmen who actually <u>pulled off</u> the heist.

   a. received

   b. removed

   c. accomplished

4. Bjoern Hoen was <u>convicted</u> of planning the robbery and sentenced to seven years in jail.

    a. found guilty

    b. declared innocent

    c. praised for

5. Soon after the theft, the getaway car was recovered and police discovered some <u>evidence</u>.

    a. unusual objects of art

    b. information used to prove guilt or innocence

    c. remarkable accomplishments

6. Maybe they <u>got away with it</u> after all.

    a. avoided punishment

    b. were sent to jail

    c. painted the pictures

7. Many people feared that the <u>irreplaceable</u> masterpieces had been lost forever.

    a. difficult to place

    b. easily replaceable

    c. not able to be replaced

B. *Complete each sentence with a two-word verb from the list.*

pull through   pull for
pull together   pull out
pull over

1. The police officer told the man to _____ because he was driving a stolen car.

2. After the paintings were stolen, police from all over the city _____ to help each other find them.

3. After a long negotiation about the price of the painting, the owner of the art gallery decided to _____ of the deal. He decided the painting was too expensive.

4. John's surgery was long and difficult, but the doctors assured us that he would

_____.

5. Good luck, Jose. I hope your painting is chosen for the show. We're

_____ you.

UNIT 7   TEST

Read the article.

The Martians Are Coming

One of the most famous radio broadcasts in history took place at 8:00 P.M. on October 30, 1938. On this quiet Sunday night, over 32 million Americans sat down by their radios to listen to their favorite shows. It was the night before Halloween, and many decided to listen to a popular program starring Orson Welles. The program that evening was an adaptation of a science fiction story called *The War of the Worlds*. Welles thought that this story about a Martian invasion of Earth would be a good one for the night before Halloween because it was scary. To make the story more realistic, Welles made some changes to the original story. For example, he changed the setting from London in the 1890s to present-day New Jersey. He also told the story as a series of news flashes that interrupted what sounded like a normal musical program.

An announcer had stated at the beginning of the show that the program was a fictional dramatization. Unfortunately, many listeners tuned in after the show had begun and missed the announcement. They were shocked and afraid when they heard that Martians had landed in the United States. They thought they were listening to a real news bulletin.

The show began with an orchestra playing dance music. After a few minutes, the music was interrupted with a "news bulletin" reporting that astronomers had just seen explosions of gas coming from the planet Mars. The broadcast returned to the music program, but soon it was interrupted again with more news. This time a large meteor had struck Earth, landing on a farm near Grovers Mill, New Jersey. A reporter was soon there to describe the strange scene, and the broadcast now switched over to continuous coverage of this rapidly unfolding story. Throughout the rest of the show, actors pretending to be reporters and policemen monitored the situation. They described the terrifying event in great detail.

To the dismay of the terrified audience listening to the broadcast, the events around the Grovers Mill meteor quickly moved from the strange to the frightening. It turned out that the meteor was not a meteor. It was, in fact, some kind of spaceship. When the spaceship opened, Martians, driving huge fighting machines and armed with strange devices that sprayed poison gas, emerged. They were moving on New York City. Soon they learned that smoke was covering New York City. Here's what listeners heard:

> Smoke comes out . . . black smoke, drifting over the city. People in the streets see it now. They're running toward the East River . . . thousands of them, dropping like rats. Now the smoke's spreading faster. It's reached Times Square. People are trying to run away from it, but it's no use. They're falling like flies. Now the smoke's crossing Sixth Avenue . . . Fifth Avenue . . . one hundred yards away . . . it's fifty feet . . .

Soon it was apparent that thousands of frightened Americans believed that an actual invasion of Earth was taking place. The program was so realistic that they thought they could really hear the Martians and smell their poison gas. Acting on the misconception that the broadcast was real, some people packed their suitcases, got into their cars, and attempted to escape. Others tried to defend themselves from the aliens by hiding in basements, loading guns, even wrapping their heads in wet towels to protect themselves from Martian poison gas.

For Your Information 4 Teacher's Manual   **55**

Stories of panic caused by the radio show appeared all over the country. The next day, Welles held a press conference. He apologized that his broadcast had caused so many people to panic. He had not anticipated such a strong reaction to the show. Today we are much more aware of the power of the media to manipulate an audience.

Part 1 *(13 points)*

A. *Circle the correct answer.*

1. The article mainly discusses _____ .

    a. a real Martian invasion

    b. a radio broadcast that caused many people to panic

    c. how to protect yourself from poison gas

    d. the life of Orson Welles

2. Where does the author describe some people's reaction to the program?

    a. paragraph 2

    b. paragraph 3

    c. paragraph 5

    d. paragraph 6

3. Where does the author discuss two changes Welles made in the original story so that his broadcast would seem more realistic?

    a. paragraph 1

    b. paragraph 2

    c. paragraph 3

    d. paragraph 4

4. What is the tone of the article?

    a. humorous

    b. scary

    c. nostalgic

    d. informative

B. *Check the statements you can infer based on the information in the article.*

_____ **1.** The original *War of the Worlds* was set in London in the late nineteenth century.

_____ **2.** Radio broadcasts can be made to sound very realistic.

_____ **3.** Martians use poison gas as a weapon.

_____ **4.** Orson Welles was sorry for the panic his show had caused.

_____ **5.** Most Americans are still afraid of invasions from other planets.

_____ **6.** Broadcasting can have a powerful effect on its audience.

_____ **7.** Everyone in the United States had a radio by 1930.

_____ **8.** A large meteor struck Earth on October 30, 1938.

_____ **9.** Scary stories are popular on Halloween.

Part 2 *(11 points)*

A. *Complete each sentence with a word from the list.*

> misconception   anticipated
> apparent   monitor
> device

1. It soon became _____ that no one understood the lesson.

2. We need someone to _____ the situation before it gets out of hand.

3. It's a _____ that older people have more difficulty learning how to use new technology.

4. We should have _____ the impact the story would have on the audience.

5. Scientists use a special _____ for measuring very small distances.

B. *Circle the correct word to complete each sentence.*

1. Did you (memory / memorize) the words to the song?

2. You need to (adjust / adjustable) the volume of your radio.

3. We are going to (observe / observable) the effect of the media.

4. His goal is challenging, but I think it is (achieve / achievable).

5. *The War of the Worlds* broadcast caused (terror / terrorize) throughout the country.

6. This magazine is a (rely / reliable) source of news.

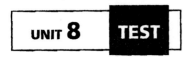

Read the article.

Big Blunders from Big Business

International marketing can be a tricky business. With the increase in global trade, international companies cannot afford to make costly advertising mistakes if they want to be competitive and profitable. Understanding the language of target markets in foreign countries is crucial to any successful international business endeavor.

Faulty Translations

The value of understanding the language of a country cannot be overestimated. Translation mistakes can result in blunders in international advertising. Since a language is more than the sum of its words, a literal, word-by-word dictionary translation rarely works. The following examples prove this point.

Otis Elevator Company once displayed a poster at a trade show in Moscow that surprised people. Due to a poor translation of its message, the sign boasted that the firm's equipment was great for improving a person's sex life.

The Parker Pen Company suffered an embarrassing moment when it realized that a faulty translation of one of its ads into Spanish resulted in a promise to "help prevent unwanted pregnancies."

Automobile manufacturers from the United States have made several notorious advertising mistakes. General Motors learned a costly lesson when it introduced its Chevrolet Nova to the Puerto Rican market. Although *nova* means "star" in Spanish, when it is spoken, it sounds like *no va*, which means "it doesn't go." Few people wanted to buy a car with that meaning. When GM changed the name to Caribe, sales increased. Ford also ran into trouble with the name of one of its products. When it introduced a low-cost truck called the Iera into Spanish-speaking countries, Ford didn't realize until too late that the name means "ugly old woman" in Spanish. Another American auto manufacturer made a mistake when it translated its Venezuelan ad for a car battery. It was no surprise when Venezuelan customers didn't want to buy a battery that was advertised as being "highly overrated."

Airline companies have also experienced problems of poor translation. A word-by-word translation ruined a whole advertising campaign for a major airline company. Hoping to promote its comfortable leather seats, an ad urged passengers to "fly on leather." However, when the slogan was translated into Spanish, it told customers to "fly naked." Another airline company made a similar mistake when it translated its motto "We earn our wings daily" into Spanish. The poor translation suggested that its passengers often ended up dead.

Marketing blunders have also been made by food and beverage companies. One American food company's friendly Jolly Green Giant became something quite different when it was translated into Arabic as "Intimidating Green Ogre." When translated into German, Pepsi's popular slogan "Come alive with Pepsi" came out implying "Come alive from the grave." No wonder customers in Germany didn't rush out to buy Pepsi. Even a company with an excellent international track record like Kentucky Fried Chicken can make mistakes. It lost a lot of sales when the slogan "finger-lickin' good" became "eat your fingers off" in the Chinese translation.

Preventing Blunders

Today companies are paying more attention to accurate translations of their ads. The best way to avoid mistakes is to hire trained professional translators who understand the target language and its idiomatic usage. Many international companies are using a technique called "back translation," which greatly reduces the risk of advertising blunders. The process of back translation requires one person to translate the message into the target language. Then another person translates the new version back into the original language. The purpose is to determine whether the original material and the retranslated material are the same. In this way companies can ensure that their intended message is really being conveyed.

Effective translators aim to capture the overall message of an advertisement because a word-for-word duplication of the original rarely conveys the intended meaning and often causes misunderstandings. In designing ads to be used in other countries, marketers should keep messages as short and simple as possible and avoid idioms and slang that are difficult to translate. Similarly, they should avoid jokes, since humor does not translate well from one culture to another. What is considered funny in one part of the world may not be humorous in another country. It could even be offensive. The bottom line is that consumers interpret advertising in terms of their own cultures. As the global marketplace opens up, there is no room for linguistic blunders.

Part 1 *(12 points)*

*Read these statements. If a statement is true, write **T** on the line. If it is false, write **F**.*

_____ 1. Understanding the language of target markets is important in doing business internationally.

_____ 2. Word-by-word translations are often inaccurate.

_____ 3. Companies shouldn't waste money on using trained translators.

_____ 4. Food and beverage companies have never experienced problems of poor translation of ads.

_____ 5. Idioms and slang are usually easy to translate.

_____ 6. Marketers should use jokes in their advertisements.

_____ 7. The process of back translation involves two people.

_____ 8. Consumers interpret advertising in terms of their own cultures.

_____ 9. Back translation tends to increase the possibility of advertising blunders.

_____ 10. Many popular slogans don't translate well into other languages.

_____ 11. Venezuelan customers rushed to buy a battery advertised as being "highly overrated."

_____ 12. Successful translators capture the overall message of an advertisement.

Part 2 *(13 points)*

A. *Read each pair of words. Write an **S** if they are synonyms. Write an **A** if they are antonyms. (1 point each)*

1. accurate   faulty   _____

2. crucial   unimportant   _____

3. blunder   mistake   _____

4. appropriate   unacceptable   _____

5. boasted   claimed   _____

6. endeavor   venture   _____

7. offensive   rude   _____

B. *Circle the correct word to complete each sentence.*

1. The faulty translation of the ad (affected / effected) sales.

2. The sales promotion worked well in most European countries (accept / except) Spain.

3. The (principle / principal) reason the advertising campaign failed was the faulty translation of its slogan.

4. We spent a whole (weak / week) working on the poster for the trade show.

5. Do you know (who's / whose) dictionary this is?

6. We decided not to (precede / proceed) with the sales campaign after all.

UNIT TESTS ANSWER KEY

UNIT 1 TEST

Part 1 A
1. T
2. T
3. F
4. F
5. T
6. T
7. F

Part 1 B
1. Opinion
2. Fact
3. Fact
4. Opinion
5. Fact
6. Opinion

Part 2 A
1. b
2. a
3. c

Part 2 B
1. c
2. e
3. a
4. f
5. b
6. d

Part 2 C
1. educational
2. suggestion
3. respond

UNIT 2 TEST

Part 1 A
1. c
2. a
3. b

Part 1 B
1.
2.
3. ✓

4.
5. ✓
6. ✓
7.
8.
9. ✓

Part 2 A
1. b
2. a
3. b
4. a
5. a
6. c
7. b

Part 2 B
1. misbehave
2. miscounted
3. mistrust
4. misunderstood
5. misguided

UNIT 3 TEST

Part 1 A
1. F
2. T
3. F
4. T
5. T
6. F
7. T

Part 1 B
1. b
2. a
3. c
4. a

Part 2 A
1. S
2. S
3. S
4. A
5. A
6. S
7. A

Part 2 B
1. It's
2. than
3. lose
4. there
5. too
6. quiet
7. their

UNIT 4 TEST

Part 1 A
1. T
2. F
3. F
4. T
5. T
6. T

Part 1 B
Order of events: 5, 7, 3, 4, 1, 2, 6

Part 2 A
1. b
2. a
3. c

Part 2 B
1. A
2. S
3. S

Part 2 C
1. exist*ence*
2. perform*ance*
3. accept*ance*

UNIT 5 TEST

Part 1 A
1. a
2. a
3. b
4. a
5. b
6. c
7. a

8. a
9. c
10. c
11. b
12. c

Part 2 A
1. A
2. S
3. S
4. A
5. S
6. A
7. A

Part 2 B
1. a. V   b. N
2. a. N   b. V
3. a. V   b. N

UNIT 6 TEST

Part 1 A
1. $300,000
2. Petter Tharaldsen
3. August 2004
4. $6.4 million
5. Iver Stensrud
6. *Madonna*

Part 1 B
1. T
2. F
3. F
4. T
5. F
6. F
7. T

Part 2 A
1. b
2. a
3. c
4. a
5. b
6. a
7. c

Part 2 B
1. pull over
2. pull together
3. pull out
4. pull through
5. pulling for

UNIT 7 TEST

Part 1 A
1. b
2. c
3. a
4. d

Part 1 B
1. ✓
2. ✓
3.
4. ✓
5.
6. ✓
7.
8.
9. ✓

Part 2 A
1. apparent
2. monitor
3. misconception
4. anticipated
5. device

Part 2 B
1. memorize
2. adjust
3. observe
4. achievable
5. terror
6. reliable

UNIT 8 TEST

Part 1 A
1. T
2. T
3. F
4. F
5. F
6. F
7. T
8. T
9. F
10. T
11. F
12. T

Part 2 A
1. A
2. A
3. S
4. A
5. S
6. S
7. S

Part 2 B
1. affected
2. except
3. principal
4. week
5. whose
6. proceed

STUDENT BOOK
ANSWER KEY

UNIT 1

CHAPTER 1

Comprehension Check

A (page 5)

1.	T	6.	F
2.	T	7.	T
3.	F	8.	T
4.	T	9.	T
5.	F		

B (page 5)

Answers may vary.
1. to the United States
2. she was 15 years old
3. no English
4. learned/become fluent in English
5. several awards
6. to speak at her graduation
7. wrote a book
8. *Looking for Trouble*
9. her experiences
10. other people learning a new language
11. all right to make mistakes
12. go to Stanford University

Vocabulary Practice

A (page 6)

1.	b	6.	a
2.	b	7.	c
3.	a	8.	a
4.	c	9.	b
5.	b		

B (page 7)

1. exhausting
2. specific
3. wild
4. hesitant
5. delighted
6. defeat
7. unusual
8. humor
9. received

C (page 8)

1. dangerous
2. general
3. adventurous
4. embarrassed
5. valuable
6. fear
7. developed
8. accomplishment
9. confused

D (page 8)

1. valuable
2. developed
3. dangerous
4. embarrassed
5. accomplishment
6. fears
7. adventurous

Reading about Scientific Research (page 9)

1. Neuroscientist Joy Hirsch and graduate student Karl Kim
2. Memorial Sloan-Kettering Cancer Center in New York
3. The brains of two groups of bilingual people: (1) people who had learned a second language as children and (2) people who had learned their second language later in life.
4. Wernicke's area and Broca's area
5. Children and adults do not use the same parts of the brain when learning a second language.
6. a. When language is being hard-wired in children, the brain combines sounds and structures from all languages into the same area. But after that wiring is complete, the management of a new language must be taken over by a different part of the brain.
   b. Children and adults may acquire languages differently.

CHAPTER 2

Before You Read

A (page 11)

1, 2, 4, 5, 6

Comprehension Check

A (page 14)

1.	F	7.	T
2.	F	8.	F
3.	F	9.	T
4.	F	10.	T
5.	T	11.	T
6.	T	12.	F

Vocabulary Practice

A (page 15)

1.	e	5.	g
2.	d	6.	f
3.	b	7.	c
4.	a		

B (page 15)

1. ups and downs
2. vision, artificial
3. Advocates
4. exceptions
5. participants
6. embraces

C (page 16)

1. A person who resides, or has his or her home, in a place
2. A person who examines the financial records of a company
3. A person who serves someone by doing jobs in his or her home
4. Someone who depends on you for financial support
5. Someone who opposes a particular idea or action
6. A person accused of a crime and who needs to be defended
7. Someone who assists someone else to do a job

D (page 16)

1. assistant
2. dependents
3. defendant
4. occupants
5. accountant
6. servants
7. opponents

CHAPTER 3

Before You Read

C (page 20)

1. a
2. b

Comprehension Check

A (page 23)

1. T
2. F
3. T
4. T
5. F

B (page 23)

1. b   5. a
2. c   6. b
3. a   7. c
4. b

C (page 25)

Fact: 1, 3, 5, 7
Opinion: 2, 4, 6, 8

Vocabulary Practice

A (page 25)

1. d   5. e
2. a   6. g
3. f   7. c
4. b

B (page 26)

1. abandon
2. neglected
3. submitted, sloppy
4. revitalized
5. multiple
6. alarming

C (page 26)

Verb	Noun	Adjective	Adverb
1. invent	**invention**	**inventive**	**inventively**
2. **respond**	**response**	responsive	**responsively**
3. **create**	creation	**creative**	**creatively**
4. educate	**education**	**educational**	**educationally**
5. **conclude**	**conclusion**	**conclusive**	conclusively
6. suggest	**suggestion**	suggestive	**suggestively**
7. **interact**	interaction	**interactive**	**interactively**
8. **complicate**	**complication**	complicated	
9. communicate	**communication**	**communicative**	**communicatively**

D (page 27)

1. complicated
2. conclusively
4. suggestion
5. respond
7. interact
9. creative

TIE IT ALL TOGETHER

Just for Fun (page 30)

1. b   8. c
2. k   9. j
3. a   10. f
4. d   11. e
5. m   12. n
6. l   13. i
7. g   14. h

ABC News Video Activity

B (page 31)

Suggested answers

1. Teens are more likely than adults to use abbreviations and acronyms, such as POS (parent over shoulder), when they write e-mail or text messages.
2. Baron says that using abbreviations is a form of social bonding and teens like using a code that only the "in" crowd will understand.

3. Truss thinks that this new informal language, which she calls "web-lish," is somewhere between talking and writing and that it is ruining the English language.
4. No, teens don't agree that abbreviations and acronyms are ruining the English language. Teens use this code because it makes communication faster and easier.

UNIT 2

CHAPTER 1

Comprehension Check
(page 40)

1. c   6. c
2. a   7. c
3. a   8. d
4. c   9. b
5. a   10. d

Vocabulary Practice
A (page 42)

1. predictable
2. fascinate
3. generally
4. scarcity
5. give up
6. bubbly
7. depressed
8. singular
9. believable

B (page 42)

1.	a	6.	b
2.	b	7.	a
3.	b	8.	b
4.	a	9.	a
5.	a	10.	b

C (page 43)

1. e
2. f
3. c
4. a
5. d
6. b

D (page 43)

1. twosome
2. cumbersome
3. wholesome
4. lonesome
5. tiresome
6. troublesome

CHAPTER 2

Comprehension Check

A (page 47)

1.	F	5.	T
2.	T	6.	T
3.	F	7.	F
4.	T		

Vocabulary Practice

A (page 48)

1. b
2. a
3. c
4. a
5. c
6. a
7. b
8. a
9. b
10. a

B (page 50)

1. unknown
2. no-brainer
3. wise
4. excessive
5. privilege
6. illusion
7. persist
8. exciting
9. stupid
10. fleeting

C (page 50)

1. to have doubts about the honesty or abilities of someone
2. to behave badly
3. to calculate an amount wrongly
4. to get the wrong total when you count
5. to deal with something without the necessary care or skill
6. to describe something falsely

D (page 50)

1. mishandled
2. misbehave
3. miscounted
4. mistrust
5. misrepresented
6. miscalculated

CHAPTER 3

Before You Read

B (page 52)

1, 3, 4, 6

Comprehension Check

A (page 54)

1. Red. Studies prove that the color red is a stimulant that releases adrenaline, increases the pulse rate, raises blood pressure, and enhances appetite.
2. Green
3. Yellow. It is the first color your eye processes.
4. Blue. Research shows that blue reduces appetite possibly because so few blue foods exist in nature.
5. Use small amounts of red; too much can be overwhelming.
6. Dark blue has historically been associated with power, responsibility, and respectability.

B (page 55)

Checked items: 2, 4, 5, 6

Vocabulary Practice

A (page 55)

1. a
2. a
3. b
4. b
5. b
6. a

B (page 56)

1. paint the town red
2. rolled out the red carpet
3. don't have a red cent
4. gave me the green light
5. green with envy
6. a green thumb
7. a little white lie
8. blue in the face

Choose a Title

(page 57)

3. Achieving Health, Happiness, and Success with Feng Shui

```
          [1]M [2]I  S  C  O  U  N  T
               L
      [3]G  I  L  B  E  R  T              [4]I
               U
               S                    [5]R  E  D
   [6]A  T  T  I  T  U  D  E              I
               O                    P     O
      [8]E  N  T  H  U  S  I  A  S  M
                                    R
   [9]Y     [10]B  R  I  L  L  I  A  N  T
[11]P  E           P              [12]P
 A  L  [13]A  [14]W  H  I  T  E
 S  L        W              R        A
[15]T  W  O  S  O  M  E       A       L
 E  W        S              A        E
 L     [16]G  E  O  M  A  N  C  E  R  S
           M
        [17]G  R  E  E  N
```

ABC News Video Activity

B (page 61)

Suggested answers

2. Fox's brain scans, especially of young children, show that happiness is at least partly genetic.
3. According to Dr. Lykken's thermostat analogy, a high setting means we're always cheerful like the Giggle Twins and a low setting means we are grumpy more often.
4. Dr. Lykken believes that happiness is partly genetic, but he says that we can take control and change our fixed set point of happiness by 25% or more.
5. According to Dr. Lykken, the recipe for happiness is a steady diet of little pleasures like volunteering or playing with your dog.

UNIT 3

CHAPTER 1

Comprehension Check

A (page 68)

1. a
2. b
3. c
4. a
5. c

B (page 69)

Checked items: 1, 2, 3, 7, 8

Vocabulary Practice

A (page 69)

1. c
2. e
3. f
4. b
5. a
6. d

B (page 70)

1. dreamed up
2. for the time being
3. crumble
4. swollen
5. Laundromat
6. landlord

C (page 71)

1. two
2. It's, to
3. lose
4. there
5. their
6. its
7. too
8. then

CHAPTER 2

Comprehension Check

A (page 74)

1. T
2. F
3. F
4. T
5. F
6. T
7. T
8. F

B (page 74)

1. b
2. c
3. b
4. a
5. b

Vocabulary Practice

A (page 75)

1.	h	5.	f
2.	c	6.	d
3.	a	7.	b
4.	e	8.	g

C (page 76)

1. modern
2. spacious
3. quiet
4. private
5. many
6. wonderful

CHAPTER 3

Comprehension Check

A (page 81)

1. c
2. a
3. d
4. a
5. b
6. b
7. a

C (page 83)

Vocabulary Practice

A (page 83)

1.	b	6.	a
2.	a	7.	a
3.	b	8.	b
4.	a	9.	a
5.	a		

B (page 84)

1.	S	6.	A
2.	S	7.	S
3.	A	8.	A
4.	S	9.	S
5.	S		

Reading a Short Story

C (page 87)

1.	S	6.	S
2.	M	7.	S
3.	M	8.	S
4.	M	9.	M
5.	P	10.	P

TIE IT ALL TOGETHER

ABC News Video Activity

B (page 89)

Suggested answers:
1. behavior
2. risk-takers, adventurers

3. Thomas Jefferson, Harriet Tubman, Che Guevara, Bill Gates
4. support new ideas, champion change, rebel
5. new strategies and different talents

UNIT 4

CHAPTER 1

Comprehension Check

A (page 97)

Answers may vary.
1. They teach us that success takes dedication, confidence, and hard work.
2. They can do things that most of us can't do.
3. They raise money for charities and act as mentors, talking to student groups and volunteering their time to programs that help kids stay off drugs and stay in school.
4. Because he had alcohol problems and he didn't want young people to drink.

Name	Book	Theory
1. Frank Sulloway	*Born to Rebel*	Children compete for their parents' resources. Each uses a different strategy depending on his or her birth order. Oldest children often support the status quo while younger children are more likely to be unconventional and rebellious.
2. Dalton Conley	*The Pecking Order*	Other factors (family size, economic situation, divorce, and so on) affect personality as much or more than birth order. Firstborn children are often successful because they get more resources (money and attention) from parents. As more children are born, the resources have to be divided.
3. Judith Rich Harris	*The Nurture Assumption: Why Children Turn Out the Way They Do*	Birth order cannot account for personality differences among siblings because peers outside the family are the biggest influence on children's personalities—not family relationships.

5. a. Jackie Robinson overcame racism to become the first African American to play in the modern major leagues.
    b. Wilma Rudolph survived pneumonia, scarlet fever, and polio as a child. She overcame physical challenges and rose above segregation and racism.
    c. Lance Armstrong was diagnosed with cancer but once again became the number one cyclist in the world.
6. There is more to sports than winning. Being the top scorer or having the best batting average or the fastest time are less important than giving it your best shot, whatever the outcome.
7. It takes countless hours of practice to fine-tune the skills needed to accomplish your goals.
8. It takes qualities like fairness, sportsmanship, honesty, and determination.

B (page 98)

Checked items: 2, 3, 5, 6

C (page 98)

1. a. S
    b. M
    c. S
2. a. S
    b. S
    c. M
3. a. S
    b. M
    c. S
4. a. M
    b. S
    c. S
5. a. S
    b. S
    c. M

Vocabulary Practice

A (page 99)

1. high-profile
2. distracted
3. took it in stride
4. got caught up in
5. mentor
6. perseverance
7. flaws
8. cheered
9. keep their cool

C (page 100)

1. resistance
2. absence
3. existence
4. performance
5. acceptance
6. preference
7. insurance

CHAPTER 2

Comprehension Check

A (page 104)

1. a
2. b
3. c
4. c
5. a

B (page 105)

1. 2:00 P.M. on April 10, 1896
2. Spyridon Loues
3. 2 hours, 58 minutes, 50 seconds
4. Joan Benoit Samuelson
5. 2 hours, 24 minutes, 52 seconds

6. 36
7. Argentina

C (page 106)

a. 9	g. 10
b. 3	h. 2
c. 7	i. 6
d. 1	j. 11
e. 4	k. 8
f. 5	

Vocabulary Practice

A (page 107)

1. delight
2. spectators
3. collapsed
4. triumph
5. running neck and neck
6. suspense
7. exhaustion

B (page 108)

1. f	6. e
2. i	7. c
3. d	8. a
4. h	9. b
5. g	

C (page 108)

1. out in left field
2. throw in the towel
3. ballpark figure
4. saved by the bell
5   in your corner
6. hitting below the belt
7. on the ball
8. covered all the bases
9. par for the course

D (page 109)

1. S
2. A
3. A
4. S
5. S
6. A

CHAPTER 3

Comprehension Check

A (page 115)

1. T
2. F
3. T
4. T
5. T
6. T
7. F
8. T
9. T

Vocabulary Practice

A (page 116)

1. f
2. g
3. c
4. d
5. b
6. a
7. e

B (page 116)

1. stick with it, down the road
2. equivalent
3. tactic
4. potential
5. trigger
6. consultation

C (page 117)

1. encourage
2. endanger
3. embitter
4. empower
5. enrich
6. enlarge

D (page 117)

1. embittered
2. encouraged
3. endanger
4. empowered
5. enlarged
6. enrich

Reading Poetry

(page 117)

1. optimistic, encouraging
2. Don't give up even if other people try to dissuade you.

3.–5. *Answers will vary.*

TIE IT ALL TOGETHER
Just for Fun (page 120)

ABC News Video Activity

B (page 121)

2

UNIT 5

CHAPTER 1

Comprehension Check

A (page 129)

1. F
2. F
3. T
4. F
5. T
6. F
7. T
8. T
9. T
10. F

B (page 130)

2. -Fights off infections
-Lowers blood pressure and blood sugar
-Prevents colds
-May prevent some forms of cancer, heart disease, and strokes
-May help heal stomach ulcers

S	R	X	S	Y	G	Z	H	I	Q	S	A	U	T	J	W	K	V	A	L	M	E	N	O	O	D
T	A	D	V	X	A	M	E	R	D	W	C	R	A	A	R	A	N	L	A	Z	Y	T	R	B	I
L	S	K	I	N	G	I	N	S	I	B	E	C	E	V	O	L	L	E	Y	B	A	L	L	M
I	K	U	W	V	D	N	E	D	O	M	I	T	T	H	L	P	Q	R	S	G	O	O	B	S	G
N	B	B	C	Y	I	E	P	S	I	M	B	O	F	T	E	Z	Q	R	L	S	L	A	N	N	H
G	L	K	F	G	I	N	I	N	N	I	S	O	M	O	B	R	C	R	W	L	M	A	I	I	L
D	C	A	J	H	K	L	G	O	O	N	Y	T	A	B	C	O	Y	E	A	T	G	L	Y	K	K
H	O	R	S	E	R	A	C	I	N	G	Z	H	E	X	Y	C	R	B	L	E	C	D	R	I	J
M	J	A	P	O	S	V	U	L	T	O	R	E	D	E	O	R	T	I	U	Y	C	D	E	E	F
O	E	T	Q	R	W	U	T	W	I	L	L	I	T	V	B	E	U	I	C	C	J	U	D	O	G
I	C	E	S	K	A	T	I	N	G	I	S	O	B	P	K	W	K	I	B	T	I	F	Y	I	E
F	P	X	Y	Z	A	Z	E	B	R	A	T	T	R	S	O	Z	B	O	S	J	A	O	J	A	A
H	R	I	E	B	O	B	O	Y	S	I	J	S	A	T	I	T	H	O	C	K	E	Y	T	I	B
Q	G	C	E	N	O	P	O	P	I	S	R	B	E	G	A	D	E	C	F	B	E	Y	O	N	C
S	T	B	A	S	E	B	A	L	L	O	O	B	O	T	L	A	D	F	U	G	E	T	I	N	D

3. -Prevents nausea
  -Aids digestion
  -Relaxes blood vessels and
   stimulates blood flow
  -Lowers blood pressure and
   reduces blood clotting
  -Stimulates blood
   circulation and reduces
   fever
  -Fights colds and cleanses
   the kidneys
  -Soothes painful joints and
   cures skin infections
4. -Prevents tooth decay
  -Fights skin and stomach
   cancer
  -Helps the immune system
  -Reduces itching from
   insect bites
5. -Reduces cholesterol levels
  -Helps lower blood
   pressure
  -Limits the risk of diseases
   of the blood vessels

Vocabulary Practice

A (page 130)

1.	a	6.	b
2.	a	7.	a
3.	a	8.	a
4.	b		
5.	b		

B (page 131)

1.	A	5.	S
2.	S	6.	S
3.	S	7.	S
4.	S	8.	A

C (page 132)

1. very poor, without any
   money
2. brave, without any fears
3. lacking power
4. not having any children
5. unable to speak or think
   of something to say

CHAPTER 2

Before You Read

B (page 133)

1. a
2. a
3. b

Comprehension Check

A (page 137)

1. b
2. b
3. c
4. b
5. a
6. b
7. c

B (page 138)

Name	Occupation	Quote
1. Dr. Clyde L. Nash	Doctor	**"Music reduces tension in the operating room and also helps relax the patient. The music is better than medication."**
2. **Dr. Mathew H. M. Lee**	Doctor	"Music helps to avoid serious complications during illness. It also enhances patients' well-being and shortens their hospital stays."
3. Janet Lapp	**Psychologist**	"Music can be very helpful for people who suffer from migraine headaches."
4. Deforia Lane	Music therapist	**"Music is not magic. . . . But in a hospital or at home, for young people or older ones, it can be a potent medicine that helps us all."**
5. Ruthlee Adler	**Music therapist**	"While the seriously handicapped may ignore other kinds of stimulation, they respond to music."
6. **Oliver Sacks**	Neurologist	"The power of music is remarkable in [patients with neurological disorders]."
7. **Jeffrey Scheffel**	Research administrator	**"It gives my brain a break, lets me focus on something else for a few minutes, and helps me get through the rest of the day."**
8. **Nathan A. Berger**	Doctor	"Music can also act as a tension- or pain-reliever for something as routine as going to the dentist. . . . or it can simply give expression to our moods."

Vocabulary Practice

A (page 139)

1. removed from
2. feeling worse
3. moderate
4. forgets
5. primary
6. out of order
7. theory
9. ordinary

B (page 140)

1.	a	5.	a
2.	b	6.	b
3.	a	7.	b
4.	b	8.	a

C (page 140)

1.	d	4.	a
2.	c	5.	d
3.	b	6.	c

CHAPTER 3

Before You Read

B (page 142)

b.

Comprehension Check

A (page 144)

1.	a	5.	b
2.	d	6.	b
3.	d	7.	c
4.	a	8.	a

C (page 147)

1. Scientists and doctors study frogs because frogs and toads have devised unique chemical adaptations that make them valuable helpers in the search for new, more effective medicines.
2. Female Queensland frogs swallowed their eggs to protect them from predators.
3. The research on Queensland frogs ended because the frogs become extinct in 1980.

4. They produce bad-tasting chemicals to protect themselves from predators. The chemicals make them extremely unpalatable to predators.
5. Scientists are studying the endangered Houston toad because it produces a chemical that may help people with heart problems.

Vocabulary Practice

A (page 147)

1.	d	5.	a
2.	c	6.	g
3.	e	7.	b
4.	f	8.	h

C (page 148)

1. a. to make/verb
   b. products of farms and gardens, mainly fruits and vegetables/noun
2. a. to help or be useful to someone/verb
   b. a helpful or good effect/noun
3. a. covered with something/verb
   b. an outer piece of clothing worn for warmth/noun
4. a. mentioned/verb
   b. a short piece of writing/noun
5. a. deep injuries to the skin/noun
   b. twisted/verb

Read a Prescription Label

(page 149)

1. Sansom Street Pharmacy
2. Dr. Steven Marks
3. Lipitor
4. Samuel Roth
5. 30
6. daily (every day)
7. 2005112

TIE IT ALL TOGETHER

Just for Fun (page 152)

ABC News Video Activity

B (page 153)

Suggested answers

2. Matthew's piano talent is especially amazing because he memorizes notes well and has the ability to improvise when playing the jazz greats.

3. Matthew's parents believe that his ability to play the piano is related to a condition that accompanies his autism and causes him to fixate on words and numbers.

4. Matthew earns money for his performances, but his parents do not tell him this for fear he will become obsessed with playing for money.

5. In addition to playing the jazz classics very well, part of what makes Matthew's talent so unusual is the adult sensitivity he brings to each performance.

UNIT 6

CHAPTER 1

Comprehension Check

A (page 161)

1. T
2. T
3. F
4. F
5. F
6. T
7. F
8. F

B (page 162)

1. Milton Esterow
2. Huntington Block
3. William E. Martin
4. James D. Keith
5. Anne Hawley

C (page 162)

1. 2004
2. 10,000
3. Milton Esterow
4. 1988
5. *Dr. No*

Vocabulary Practice

A (page 162)

1. ransom
2. confessed
3. guilty
4. convicted
5. pulled off
6. evidence
7. legitimate
8. obscure
9. penalties

B (page 164)

1. obscure
2. prize
3. unlawful
4. failed
5. painting
6. deny
7. approved
8. question

C (page 164)

1. pulled together
2. pull out
3. pull over
4. pull through
5. pulling for

CHAPTER 2

Before You Read

B (page 166)
Checked items: 1, 3, 4, 5, 8

Comprehension Check

A (page 169)

1. F   5. F
2. T   6. T
3. T   7. T
4. T

B (page 170)
Answers may vary.

1. a machine to catch people who are carrying explosives; special software to match a document with the printer that printed it

2. how to tell the difference between a person who has drowned and a person who has been strangled

3. clues about how someone died and about how a person lived

4. help put dangerous criminals in jail; solve mysteries that have been around for decades; save lives or bring peace to families who have lost a loved one

Vocabulary Practice

A (page 170)

1. c   5. b
2. g   6. d
3. e   7. f
4. a

C (page 171)

1. forensic biologists— scientists who analyze blood, hair, and saliva to identify criminals

2. forensic chemists— scientists who look at powders and other materials for traces of drugs or explosives

3. forensic anthropologists— scientists who study bones to estimate how old people were when they died

4. forensic meteorologists— scientists who track weather patterns

CHAPTER 3

Comprehension Check

A (page 175)

1. c
2. a
3. b
4. d
5. b
6. d

B (page 176)

1. Jamie Rappaport Clark
2. $40
3. 71 months
4. TRAFFIC
5. rhinoceros horns and tiger bones
6. Guy Richardson

C (page 176)

1. illegal animal trade
2. several billion dollars
3. poachers
4. dealers
5. smuggle the animals
6. catch and punish poachers, traders, and smugglers
7. Keng Liang Wong
8. hurts precious creatures
9. hurts the habitats they leave behind

Vocabulary Practice

A (page 177)

1. c
2. h
3. b
4. d
5. g
6. a
7. f
8. e

B (page 177)

1. traffic
2. on the brink of
3. poachers
4. smuggled
5. tracked down
6. dreadful
7. concealed
8. crack down on

C (page 178)

il-: illiterate, illegible
ir-: irrelevant, irreplaceable
im-: improbable, immature
in-: invisible, incomplete

TIE IT ALL TOGETHER

Just for Fun (page 180)

1. The airline clerk had sold the lawyer only one round-trip ticket to Switzerland and also one one-way ticket.
2. It was still daylight.
3. Throw it up in the air.

4. They make more money cutting the hair of ten men than cutting the hair of one.

ABC News Video Activity

B (page 181)

1. surrounding them with their scent
2. protect the elephants from poachers who want to kill them for their ivory tusks
3. at night
4. an elephant orphanage in Kenya
5. elephants will continue to be in danger

UNIT 7

CHAPTER 1

Comprehension Check

A (page 189)

1. c
2. d
3. b
4. c
5. b
6. b
7. d
8. c

B (page 190)

See sample answers in the chart below and continued on page 77. Answers may vary.

Device/Procedure	Space Use/Description	Practical Application
sight switch	lets astronauts control their spacecraft without using arms and legs	permits handicapped people to operate devices they could not otherwise use
voice command device	enables astronauts to steer their spacecraft by voice command	helps deaf people learn to speak
small television cameras	miniature electronic instruments small enough and durable enough for trips into space	can be attached to a surgeon's head to give medical students a close-up view of an operation
invisible braces	strong and durable materials for spacecraft	straighten teeth

biosensors	monitor the physical signs of astronauts by checking their temperature, brain-wave activity, breathing rate, and heartbeat	send data by wire or radio, which are displayed on computer screens for doctors to analyze
special bed	for astronauts to sleep on	used for burn patients; enables them to float on a cushion of air so burns can heal more quickly because they do not rub against the bed
special stretcher	removes injured workers from the huge propellant tanks of the *Saturn V* rocket	removes injured workers from mines, oil-drilling rigs, and boats
smoke detector	first used in NASA's first space station, Skylab	use in homes
cordless tools	used by the Apollo astronauts to drill into the moon's surface and collect soil and rock samples to bring back to Earth	home repair
fiberglass materials	created for rocket-fuel tanks	used to make very strong and durable storage tanks, railway tank cars, and highway tankers
magnetic hammer	eliminated small imperfections in the *Saturn V* rocket	used in the automotive and shipbuilding industries
spacesuits	clothing for astronauts	clothing for other professions such as firefighter suits with "fireblocking" materials that are more resistant to cracking and burning; thermal gloves and socks to keep hands and feet warm
spacers	ventilation and cushioning in moon boots	used in athletic shoes that are designed to reduce fatigue and injury
quartz timing crystals	highly accurate, lightweight, and durable timing device for the *Apollo* spacecraft	used in watches and clocks
bar codes	a way to keep track of millions of spacecraft parts	used by stores and manufacturers to keep track of sales and stock
systems approach	brings together all the elements of a complex project to assure that everything is completed at the optimum time	used in cancer research, hospital design, city planning, crime detection, pollution control, building construction, and transportation

Vocabulary Practice

A (page 191)

1. d
2. h
3. c
4. e
5. a
6. g
7. b
8. f

B (page 191)

1. a
2. b
3. a
4. b
5. b
6. a
7. a

C (page 192)

1. S
2. S
3. A
4. A
5. S
6. A
7. S
8. S

D (page 192)

1. specialize
2. memorize
3. symbolize
4. agonize
5. finalize
6. modernize

CHAPTER 2

Before You Read

B (page 194)

1. b
2. a
3. c

Comprehension Check

A (page 197)

1. the director of the Mars Gravity Biosatellite Program at the Massachusetts Institute of Technology
2. radio-controlled robots, or rovers
3. exploring Mars
4. dealing with gravity, lack of food, water, breathable air, and extremely cold winters
5. to find out how mammals might fare on Mars
6. Water makes life possible here on Earth, so finding signs of water on Mars would indicate that life might have existed there in the past and could still be there today.

B (page 197)

Fact: 2, 3, 4, 6
Opinion: 1, 5

Vocabulary Practice

A (page 198)

1. c
2. f
3. b
4. a
5. h
6. g
7. e
8. d

B (page 198)

1. gravity
2. shelter
3. ironed out
4. mission
5. collaborators
6. boost
7. composition
8. automated

C (page 199)

1. achievable
2. adjustable
3. flexible
4. enjoyable
5. identifiable
6. observable

D (page 199)

1. enjoy
2. adjust
3. flexible
4. observe
5. achievable
6. identifiable

CHAPTER 3

Comprehension Check

A (page 204)

1. a musician
2. a physicist
3. art
4. science
5. creative thinking
6. the universe
7. basic principles

B (page 204)

Checked items: 3, 4, 7

C (page 204)

Sample answers. Answers may vary.

1. Creative thinking is used in the same way in both solving a complicated mathematical problem and in painting a landscape or writing a poem or piece of music.
2. Nature and art both seem to follow certain principles.
3. Just like art and literature involve the relationships and interactions of ideas, physics involves the relationships and interactions of concepts.

Vocabulary Practice

A (page 205)

1. b
2. b
3. a
4. b
5. a
6. b
7. a
8. a

C (page 206)

1. mechanical
2. grammar
3. historical
4. mathematical
5. geography
6. medical

7. musical
8. philosophy
9. political
10. theory

D (page 206)

1. medical
2. Musical, mathematics
3. political
4. geography
5. historical
6. grammatical
7. philosophy
8. mechanical
9. theory

Learning Academic Abbreviations

(page 207)

1. Electrical Engineer
2. Doctor of Medical Dentistry
3. Master of Social Work

TIE IT ALL TOGETHER

ABC News Video Activity

B (page 209)

1. a
2. b
3. c
4. a

UNIT 8

CHAPTER 1

Before You Read

B (page 215)

1. b
2. a

Comprehension Check

(page 217)

1. T (3)
2. T (6)
3. F (11)
4. T (8)
5. T (3)

6. T (7)
7. F (9)
8. T (12)
9. F (11)
10. T (12)

Vocabulary Practice

A (page 218)

1.	b	5.	b
2.	c	6.	b
3.	c	7.	a
4.	a	8.	c

B (page 219)

1. a
2. b
3. a
4. b

Analyzing Ads

A (page 220)

Sample answers. Answers may vary.

1. Honey Hearts has all natural oat-bran flakes with honey.
2. Honey Hearts is good for your heart.
3. The calcium in the cereal will keep your teeth and bones strong.
4. There is no sugar added to the cereal.

Choose a Title

(page 221)

3. Advertising Goes Digital

CHAPTER 2

Comprehension Check

A (page 228)

Answers may vary.

1. It can weaken a company's position in the market, prevent it from accomplishing its objectives, and ultimately lead to failure.

2. They should address differences in business styles, development of business relationships, punctuality, negotiating styles, gift-giving customs, greetings, gestures, meanings of colors and numbers, and customs regarding names.

3. He or she should engage in small talk, plan a lunch or dinner, and allow time for a personal relationship to develop. Solid business opportunities usually follow a strong personal relationship in Guatemala and all of Latin America.

4. Traditional greetings include a handshake, hug, kiss, bow, and placing the hands in a praying position.

5. They can have a sensitivity to other cultures and have a good understanding of their own culture and how other countries see their culture.

B (page 229)

Answers may vary.

2. Romanians, Japanese, and Germans are very punctual, but people in Latin countries are often more casual about time.

3. When Danes hear the usual American greeting, "Hi, how are you?" they may think the U.S. businessperson really wants to know how they are.

4. The "OK" sign commonly used in the United States has several different meanings elsewhere: In France, it means zero; in Japan, it is

a symbol for money; and in Brazil, it is an offensive gesture.

5. -First names are seldom used when doing business in Germany. Visiting businesspeople should use the title and the surname.
    -Thais usually call each other by first names and use last names for very formal occasions or in writing.

6. -Gift-giving is an important part of doing business in Japan, but gifts are rarely exchanged in Germany.
    -The western tradition of accepting a business card and immediately putting it in your pocket is considered very rude in Japan, where there are social rules about how to accept a business card.

8. -A U.S. golf ball manufacturer targeted Japan as an important new market, but sales of the company's golf balls were well below average because it had packaged the balls in groups of four—the number of death in Japan.
    -Number 7 is considered bad luck in Kenya and good luck in Czech Republic and has magical connotations in Benin.
    -Red is a positive color in Denmark but represents witchcraft and death in many African countries.

C (page 230)

Answers may vary.

1. Gift-giving is an important part of doing business in Japan, but

gifts are rarely exchanged in Germany.

2. Thais address each other by first names and reserve last names for very formal occasions or in writing. However, in the U.K. it is appropriate to use titles until use of first names is suggested.

3. In the United States, the "OK" sign means okay, but in France it means zero.

4. The Japanese are very punctual. In contrast, many people in Latin countries have a more relaxed attitude toward time.

5. The number 7 is considered bad luck in Kenya. On the other hand, 7 is considered good luck in Czech Republic.

Vocabulary Practice

A (page 231)

1.	a	7.	a
2.	b	8.	b
3.	b	9.	b
4.	b	10.	b
5.	a	11.	a
6.	a		

B (page 232)

1.	S	7.	S
2	A	8.	S
3.	A	9.	S
4.	A	10.	A
5.	A	11.	A
6.	S		

C (page 233)

1. proceed
2. cite
3. affects
4. except
5. principle
6. whether
7. weak, weeks
8. whose

Choose a Title

(page 234)

1. Colors Communicate

TIE IT ALL TOGETHER

Just for Fun (page 235)

1. You would ask, "What door would the other guard tell me to use?" Then you would go through the door you were told NOT to use.

2. The Z goes above the line since the letters above the line are made up of straight lines and those below the line are made up of curved lines.

3. Daisy and Heather grow ivy and violets. Lily and Violet grow heather and roses. Rose and Ivy grow lilies and daisies.

ABC News Video Activity

B (page 236)

Sample answers. Answers way vary.

1. Food companies use popular television characters to advertise sugary cereals and unhealthy foods to children.

2. Smalls says that what's good for children is good for business.

3. Wootan says that companies will not change profitable marketing practices for altruistic reasons and that there needs to be pressure to get them to change how they advertise to children.

4. Companies stress that consumers have to be responsible for their choices and for what they eat.

THE FYI DVD PROGRAM

ABOUT THE FYI DVD PROGRAM

The DVD

The FYI 3 and 4 DVD Program includes 16 video segments featuring topics correlated to the themes in FYI Levels 3 and 4.

Scripts for Level 4

Unit 1   The IM Code
Unit 2   How to Be Happy
Unit 3   The Role of Birth Order in History
Unit 4   Barefoot Marathon
Unit 5   Matthew Savage, Jazz Pianist
Unit 6   Saving the Elephants
Unit 7   Rocket Men
Unit 8   Kids and Food

The DVD Guide

The FYI 3 and 4 DVD Guide contains unit-by-unit video scripts as well as vocabulary for comprehension and a summary statement to enhance the accessibility and enjoyment of the DVD material.

DVD Activities

Video Activities are included at the end of every Student Book unit. The activities are designed for students to use in class after watching the video segment.

Using the FYI DVD Program

Preparation

Before presenting a DVD unit to students:

1. Preview the video.

2. Read the video script, along with the summary statement and Vocabulary for Comprehension sections. You may want to take notes to plan how to prepare students for viewing the video.

Procedure

This three-phase procedure takes about 45 minutes to complete.

Before Viewing   Suggested Time: 10 minutes

1. Introduce the topic to the students. Share the background information provided in the DVD Guide or in the Student Book activity. Draw attention to how this topic relates to the theme in the FYI Student Book units.

2. Generate interest. Find out what students know about this topic and what they think they may learn.

3. Preview vocabulary. Write the words listed in the Vocabulary for Comprehension section

on the board. Review these words. Provide examples to illustrate the meanings of the remaining words. For example, use pictures, situations, synonyms, or antonyms.

Variation

You may choose to go over the meanings of the words after students have viewed the video segment for the first time and have heard the words in context.

While Viewing   **Suggested Time: 20 minutes**

1. Have students predict. Show a short portion of the video. Use the pause control to stop the DVD. Ask students what they think the rest of the segment will be about. You may write the ideas on the board.

   Variations

   • Use the pause control to stop after a particular line of dialogue and have students predict the next line.

   • With audio off: Have students predict the content based on viewing a short segment without the sound.

   • With picture off: Have students predict what they will see by listening to the sound without watching the picture.

2. Check comprehension. Show the complete video segment. Have students answer comprehension questions you devise. Encourage students to take notes. Have students compare their answers in pairs and then share them as a class. If students demonstrate a desire to view the video in order to clarify a question, show that particular portion of the video.

   Variations

   • Freeze-frame the entire video segment frame-by-frame by using the pause button and check students' understanding.

   • For detailed listening comprehension practice, copy and distribute a portion of the video script with selected words blanking out. Have students fill in the missing words.

After Viewing   **Suggested Time: 15 minutes**

1. Share reactions and opinions on the topic. Go back to the ideas students generated before viewing the video. Were their predictions accurate?

2. Consider some of the suggested activities below.

Speaking Activities

• Oral summary: Have students work in pairs to summarize the content of the video. Have pairs present their summaries to the class.

• Role play: Give students various roles of people portrayed in the video. Have students improvise conversations, interviews, or panel discussions based on what they saw in the video.

• Debate: Have students examine both sides of an issue raised in the video. Divide the class into two groups, pro and con, and have the groups present contrasting viewpoints.

• Critical review: Have students review the video segment as critics. Have them describe what they liked or didn't like, and what they would change and why.

• Oral research report: Have students search in the library or on the Internet for more information on the person, place, or issue covered in the video and present an oral report to the class.

• Survey: Have each student create an opinion or personal experience question related to the topic in the video. Have students circulate and ask each other their questions. Report results to the whole class.

Writing Activities

- Note taking: Have students practice note-taking skills as they watch the video segment.

- Paraphrasing: Have students paraphrase selected portions of the video script.

- Summarizing: Have students write a short summary of the video segment. Encourage students to use terms from the Vocabulary for Comprehension section.

- Expository writing: Have students write about an aspect of the video topic that interests them or that they agree or disagree with.

- Critical review: Have students write a review of the video segment. Have them describe what they liked or disliked, and what they would change and why.

- Letter: Have students write a letter to one of the "experts" or people portrayed in the video segment.

- Research report: Have students search in the library or on the Internet for more information on the person, place, or issue covered in the video segment. Have students write outlines and then complete written reports.

UNIT 1: WHAT LANGUAGES DO YOU SPEAK?

The IM Code
3:45 minutes

Anchor: Well, if this looks Greek to you, then you're behind the times because what you're seeing is the kind of language millions of people are now using to communicate. This says, "Oh my gosh! Gotta go, Talk to you later." It's fast, it's fun, and, in case you're still in the dark, Lynn Sherr has the ABCs of e-mail.

Lynn Sherr: What does that say? Oh, wait, let me try to figure this one out. WDUW2T . . . what do you want to talk about?

Hillary: Or what did you do today?

Lynn Sherr: At 16, Hillary has been tapping out little messages to her pals for seven years. Little messages most of us can't read.

Hillary: NMU is nothing about you. And then there's "sup," which is what's up.

Lynn Sherr: JC?

Hillary: Just chilling.

Lynn Sherr: It looks like an alien language. It sounds very important. It's consuming our kids and ourselves, as it elevates our thumbs to new digital equality. It's instant messaging, or IM, the teens' favored tool. Text messaging, the shortened slang of cell phones. And grown-up friendly e-mail. It's predicted that by next year, more than 36 billion e-mail messages will be sent everyday. Once, communication was a long, slow process requiring quill pens and thoughtful words. But technology quickened the pace and shortened the sentences. Leading to today's lightning-fast bursts of the alphabet.

Naomi Baron: And suddenly, we learn there's a whole etiquette that becomes part of our culture.

Lynn Sherr: Naomi Baron teaches linguistics at American University. Her students can rattle off the new ABC's.

Student: RLMAO. Rolling on the floor, laughing my (censored) off.

Student: The numeral two instead of T-O.

Naomi Baron: POS, parent over shoulder.

Lynn Sherr: Baron says for kids, it's social bonding.

Naomi Baron: Well, you show you're cool by violating the conventions that you're supposed to follow in normal writing. So you don't capitalize. You say, I can throw in lots of abbreviations and acronyms that only the "in" crowd is going to understand.

Lynne Truss: It's a new form of English. It's somewhere between talking and writing.

Lynn Sherr: Which spells big trouble, says author Lynne Truss. In her best-seller, "Eats Shoots & Leaves," she frets that people have forgotten about punctuation and that e-mail and IM are ruining the English language. She calls it web-lish.

Lynne Truss: What I feel when I read something that's written all in lower case is that I'm reading something written by a 5-year-old child. And when you see a load of capitals in front, you know someone's shouting.

Lynn Sherr: And those little sideways smiley faces, emoticons, a poor substitute for words. Isn't that just the 21st century semicolon?

Lynne Truss: No, it's an ornament, but it doesn't do anything to help you with the secrets of words.

Lynn Sherr: "Oh, lighten up," say the kids. "We know the difference between cyber-speak and literature."

Hillary: We're not using this to ruin it. We're just using it because it works for us. It's AOL, like, slang, that's what it is.

Lynn Sherr: Keep in mind, this is a moving target. It will change. Meanwhile, keep learning the lingo. Tell me the sign-off.

Hillary: It's gg or g2g.

Lynn Sherr: Meaning?

Hillary: Gotta go, talk to you later, see you.

Lynn Sherr: So, tell me again what MWA is.

Hillary: It's kisses, XXO.

Lynn Sherr: Bye-bye.

UNIT 2: DON'T WORRY, BE HAPPY

How to be Happy
3:06 minutes

Michael Guillen: No one knows the ingredients for happiness better than Dr. David Lykken, professor emeritus at the University of Minnesota. Happiness is his middle—well, actually, his last name. In Norwegian, "lykken" means "the happiness." And he also just wrote the book on happiness, in which he reveals the results of a major new study on twins.

David Lykken: We found that identical twins who begin life as a single egg that divides and who therefore have the same genetic blueprint, that identical twins have very similar happiness scores.

Dr. Michael Guillen: It's as if we have a built-in happiness thermostat, says Dr. Lykken, set at the factory by our genes. A low setting means we're like the character Louis De Palma in the TV series "Taxi," always grumpy no matter what.

Danny Devito: I don't like people playing music in this garage!

Dr. Michael Guillen: A high setting means we're always cheerful, like the so-called Giggle Twins, Barbara Herbert and Daphne Goodship. Despite having been raised in totally different environments, they're both irrepressibly, irresistibly, irritatingly happy-go-lucky.

Barbara Herbert: Really do believe that it is genetic, that we are basically quite happy people.

Dr. Michael Guillen: MRIs show the left frontal lobe of a happy person's brain glows like a light bulb, the closest science has come to capturing a true picture of happiness. And at the University of Maryland, psychologist Nathan Fox says he can tell at a very early age if our happiness thermostat is set on high or low, just by looking at the vibes our brain gives off. So this is the brain pattern of what you would call an exuberant child?

Nathan Fox: These are children who are full of gusto, they are full of life.

Dr. Michael Guillen: And they're naturally that way, you find.

Nathan Fox: That's right. We start seeing them at four months of age.

Dr. Michael Guillen: So does that mean that we're genetic slaves, that we have no control

over our level of happiness? Absolutely not. For example, if you happen to be someone who inherited a low set point, who has a natural tendency to be grumpy, well, it's like saying that this bicycle has a natural tendency to pull to the right. In that case, all you have to do is grab hold, take control, and consciously make yourself happier. There's still no absolute proof, but after treating patients for 30 years, Dr. Lykken estimates you can rise above your fixed set point of happiness by 25 percent or more, starting with doing everything you can to fight off the terrible trio.

Dr. David Lykken: The three thieves of happiness that I talk about are depression, ordinary garden-variety depression, irritability, and fearfulness.

Dr. Michael Guillen: And finally, on a happiness scale of 1 to 10 Haps, don't depend on those huge 10-Hap pleasures like winning a lottery or earning that big promotion. Their high is only temporary. Instead, fill your life with a steady diet of little 1 - Hap pleasures, like volunteering your time, playing with your dog, gardening, or, in Dr. Lykken's case, baking a lemon meringue pie. Now, that, he says, is the true recipe for happiness.

Dr. David Lykken: That's good.

UNIT 3: HOME AND FAMILY

The Role of Birth Order in History
2:51 minutes

Diane Sawyer: Finally tonight, sibling rivalry. Anyone who has raised children is familiar with all the ways they compete with each other for attention, sometimes fighting, sometimes dogged achievement; to most of us, just a part of growing up. But as ABC's Robert Krulwich reports, it may also be the stuff that shapes history.

Robert Krulwich: Thirty years ago, these Supreme Court justices were actively championing racial integration, Miranda warnings for criminals. This court was the most active, controversial branch of the U.S. government. But why? What transformed the court into such a hotbed of change? One crazy possibility is suggested by a new book by scholar Frank Sulloway. He says look who was on the court in, say, 1967. It just so happens that every justice, every one, was a younger sibling, either a later child or the baby of the family. And interestingly, afterwards, when Republican presidents wanted to make the court more conservative, who did they appoint?

Ronald Reagan: Chief Justice Rehnquist and Justice Scalia.

Robert Krulwich: Well, as it happens, six of their first appointees were first borns, the oldest in their families. For 26 years, scholar Frank Sulloway has been fascinated with how birth order, where you rank in your family, affects behavior. And he says he can prove that across history, new, revolutionary ideas are resisted by first borns and supported by younger siblings. Younger siblings, he says, are the champions of change.

Frank Sulloway: They're the risk takers, the adventurers, the people who are constantly trying to find something new and different to do.

Robert Krulwich: Thomas Jefferson and Harriet Tubman and Che Guevara and Bill Gates are all later children. This is not a new notion. But Sulloway has broadened the argument by looking at particular periods which tell him, for example, that when Darwin proposed his theory of evolution, younger siblings at the time were four and a half times more supportive than first borns. When Martin Luther challenged the Catholic Church, younger siblings were 47 times more likely to fight and die in Luther's cause. Younger siblings, Sulloway argues in his new book, are born to rebel.

Frank Sulloway: It's a very striking conclusion to reach.

Robert Krulwich: And the explanation, he says, is the first child automatically gets love and status and attention from parents. But later children, to win affection, have to come up with new strategies and different talents. So younger siblings are conditioned to be more adventurous, more tolerant and experimental. So, therefore, throughout history it is the struggle between first born and younger born, Cain versus Abel. That, says Sulloway, is the struggle that has shaped our world. Robert Krulwich, ABC News.

Diane Sawyer: And we younger siblings think that's our report on World News Tonight.

UNIT 4: WINNING AND LOSING

Barefoot Marathon
2:22 minutes

Dan Harris: And finally tonight barefoot and running. Today the streets of New York City were filled with thousands of marathoners and people who came out to cheer them on. To get an extra edge, serious runners spend some serious money on high-tech shoes. It turns out they might be better off if they just kicked them off. Here's ABC's John Berman.

John Berman: 35,000 people endured the New York City marathon today. Everyday, millions more lace up their sneakers and go for a run. That, Ken Bob Saxton says, is where they all go wrong.

Ken Bob Saxton: They've lost touch, literally, with the ground.

John Berman: Ken Bob has run dozens of marathons barefoot.

Ken Bob Saxton: A lot of it is just freedom. It feels good to feel the breeze blowing across the tops of my feet.

John Berman: Not only does it feel better, but there is growing research that says it's better for you.

Irene Davis: I honestly believe we were designed to be barefoot.

John Berman: Professor Irene Davis studies running styles at the University of Delaware. She says many of the new sneakers, with all of their support, are making our feet lazy.

Irene Davis: We were really designed to have feet that help to cushion the impacts of landing. By wearing shoes, we've sort of decreased the demands on those muscles, and with time the muscles have really naturally gotten weaker.

John Berman: And that makes your feet more vulnerable to injuries. If you've worn running sneakers your whole life, like I have, it's probably not a good idea to throw out your shoes and try running barefoot right away. You have to change the way you run. Most runners strike the ground with the heels of their feet. Without shoes, that would hurt. So when barefoot, you have to land on the middle or front of your feet, with the arch helping to absorb the impact. In the lab, running barefoot, I was able to cut the shock on my shins in half.

Researcher: Perfect.

John Berman: Even sneaker giant Nike believes in some cases, less is more. Their new shoe, the Nike Free, is like a slipper with a sole, designed to be almost like going barefoot. But Ken Bob says there is no substitute for the real thing.

Ken Bob Saxton: You can tell a barefoot runner by the smile on their face.

John Berman: He says people would understand if they would just run a mile in his shoes. John Berman, ABC News, Newark, Delaware.

UNIT 5: HEALING POWER

Matthew Savage, Jazz Pianist
5:03 minutes

Bob Brown: The performance was sold out more than a week in advance for a trio featuring an innovative jazz pianist named Matt Savage. It was early afternoon because Mr. Savage, who was accompanied by veterans of the Boston area jazz scene, doesn't give late-night performances; that would keep him up way past his bedtime.

1st Man: It's so rare that you find somebody like this. That—you know, it's almost like he dropped in from another planet.

2nd Man: All I see are the feet dangling back and forth. And he's just—you know, ideas coming from the—from the piano.

Bob Brown: Matt Savage is a nine-year-old diagnosed with a form of autism which can leave a child emotionally cut off, unable to communicate well and fixated on routines. What is amazing about him, is that his ability to learn and memorize notes is accompanied by an ability to improvise classic editions of jazz and the knowledge of the techniques of great jazz musicians. What—what jazz musicians do you like to listen to?

Matthew Savage: I like Gizz—Dizzy Gillespie, Sonny Rollins, Thelonious Monk.

Bob Brown: When I talked with Matthew, I also rolled a ball back and forth with him to help keep his attention which often wanders. What kind of music do you write?

Matthew Savage: Jazz, of course.

Bob Brown: Jazz, of course. What makes jazz jazz?

Matthew Savage: The beat, the feel, the tempo, the dynamics. Now I'm going to play a tune that has been a classic for years by the early jazz great Fats Waller, entitled "Ain't Misbehavin'."

Bob Brown: But how did a child who once found music painful, learn to play like a tiny genius? His parents believe that part of it has to do with a condition that accompanies his autism called hyperlexia, an intense fixation on words and numbers that contributed to his ability to memorize music books and very quickly to read music. That started around three years ago when Matthew was six and a half. Diane showed him how the colored notes on a toy piano corresponded with tones and then helped him transfer that information to the real piano.

Diane Savage: You play the black notes. Ready? And then I brought out the music book, and I showed it to him, and he. . .

Bob Brown: He took it from you.

Diane Savage: He like grabbed it from me and he just sat there and read it from—from cover to cover, and he would—played every single song in there.

Bob Brown: Matthew loved to improvise which amazed the musicians who heard him and led Diane and Larry to get him teachers both for jazz and classical music. He still fixates on things, still has obsessions and distractions.

Matthew Savage: This is my second window.

Bob Brown: But he functions at a much higher level than he did when he was younger. And he has a sense of humor that's apparent in the titles of the jazz compositions he writes. "Summer Fever" and "Shufflin' the Cards." He starts off other musicians in his own inimitable way.

Diane Savage: The funniest was, and it was at his last concert and Matthew just said, 'A one, a two, and you know what to do.'

Bob Brown: Is he earning money as a musician now?

Larry Savage: He's starting to, yeah.

Bob Brown: Do—does he know that he's making money?

Diane Savage: No, and—and that's purposeful. He fixates on things like the lottery or "Wheel of Fortune." And I'm very much afraid that if he knows that he can make money by playing music, then that's going to be an obsession for him.

Bob Brown: Only God knows what's in his mind when he plays a Thelonious Monk ballad with an adult sensitivity in the span of his nine-year-old fingers. His future is impossible to predict, and the well-spring of his talent may be a mystery to us, but to him it is as simple and profound as it is for all musicians. It makes him happy when he plays.

Matthew Savage: I feel really involved in the music. I feel happy.

UNIT 6: CRIME

Saving the Elephants
2:15 minutes

Martin Seemungal: They are majestic and powerful. They seem invincible. But just watch how vulnerable they are when man is around. These men know exactly how to kill elephants. They circle the herd, always downwind, so the elephants can't immediately pick up their scent. When the elephants can finally smell the humans, it's too late. The scent is all around. The herd doesn't know which way to run. So if we were poachers, it would have been easy to get them?

Habil Olembo: Yeah, we would have just killed all of them, yeah.

Martin Seemungal: But these men did not come to kill elephants, they're here to protect them from poachers who want their tusks. Poaching has increased since the announcement of next year's one-time sale of legally-stockpiled ivory. That sale, these men fear, will allow smugglers to pass off ivory from elephants like these as legal.

Peter Leitoroh: The threat is there. It's a reality, because it's, it's an armed gangs we are dealing with.

Martin Seemungal: Which is why these park rangers are here. The rangers have been watching over the elephants off and on throughout the day. Now, it's nightfall. And things are about to get a lot more dangerous. These rangers know that poachers nearly always strike at night. They are heavily armed. And this park is about the size as the state of Michigan. There are other anti-poaching patrols out tonight. But they cannot guard all the elephants in the park. One day last year, the harsh morning sun revealed this killing field. The entire herd wiped out.

Daphne Sheldrick: When they greet one another, they use their trunk.

Martin Seemungal: Baby elephants don't have tusks and often survive the poachers' guns. The rangers bring them to the Sheldrick Center at the Nairobi National Park. Daphne Sheldrick has been running the elephant orphanage here for over 20 years.

Daphne Sheldrick: As long as there's an ivory trade sanctioned, the elephants are going to be under serious threat.

Martin Seemungal: Kenya's Wildlife Service killed four poachers last year and arrested several others. Night after night, they lay traps like this, waiting to ambush the poachers. They say the question is not will the poachers come, it's a matter of when. Martin Seemungal, ABC News, Tsavo, Kenya.

UNIT 7: THE UNIVERSE AND BEYOND

Rocket Men
2:07 minutes

Dean Reynolds: Burt Rutan is a man in a hurry.

Burt Rutan: I'm going to do future things as quickly as I can. I've got a lot of gray hair already, and I want to go to the planets.

Dean Reynolds: Rutan built the first plane to fly nonstop around the world and hopes his newest invention goes beyond it.

Burt Rutan: We've left it to NASA for 42 years, okay? And there's been only 241 manned space flights in 42 years.

Dean Reynolds: Rutan says it's time for private companies to step in and get a piece of the action. And he's not alone. There are now more than 20 private teams competing to be the first to finance, build and launch a manned space vehicle, something that would win them the X-Prize, a $10 million jackpot for the first to send up to three people into suborbital flight, about 62 miles up, and then do it again within two weeks. Up and back, the flight would last only 15 minutes, but it's a first 4,000 mile an hour step toward commercial space travel.

Steve Bennett: My dream is to open the space frontier to allow ordinary people to be able to fly or holiday in space.

Dean Reynolds: Steve Bennett's Starchaser is being tested in Britain. He sees a day when private carriers ship cargo around the solar system, a day when tourists tumble-roll their way to weekends at space hotels.

Steve Bennett: There's a whole new industry about to open up. We're going to be at the forefront of that industry.

Dean Reynolds: And there's no shortage of would-be astronauts.

Brian Wendt: That was actually part of my career plans, at least, sort of the far out type of career plans.

Dean Reynolds: Brian Wendt has flown only small planes and only for a couple of years at that, but he's undaunted.

Brian Wendt: I get to ride on a cool vehicle and go up into space and maybe start a new industry.

Dean Reynolds: Right now, some competitors would appear to have a bit of an edge on others, whose reach may well exceed their grasp. But one Canadian team says it may be ready for launch later this year, and who knows what happens then. After all, the sky's the limit. Dean Reynolds, ABC News, Chicago.

UNIT 8: BUSINESS SAVVY

Kids and Food
2:36 minutes

Elizabeth Vargas: We're going to take "A Closer Look" this evening at a new effort to tackle childhood obesity. This generation of children is the heaviest in American history. An estimated 16 percent of all children and teenagers are overweight, four times as many since the 1960s. In Washington today, the government brought together companies in the business of food and media to talk about how they can address the problem, on their own, without new regulations. But will voluntary measures by the companies be enough? Here's ABC's Lisa Stark.

Lisa Stark: Some of the most popular children's TV characters will soon be assuming new roles. Nickelodeon will put SpongeBob, Dora the Explorer and the dog, Blue, on everything from carrots to spinach to milk cartons.

Marva Smalls: We learned very early on that what's good for kids is good for business.

Lisa Stark: Increasingly, companies are under pressure to encourage healthy eating. Ronald McDonald has a new exercise habit. Red Lobster offers kids' meals with steamed vegetables. And Kraft no longer advertises some of its most sugary cereals to kids. Market researchers say this trend will continue.

Brady Darvin: This time, it's going to stick, because attitudes are changing as a result of all of the media attention that the obesity epidemic has gotten.

Lisa Stark: And today's high-profile meeting in Washington, a warning for those in the business of marketing to children.

Deborah Platt Majoras: We believe a government ban on children's food advertising is neither wise nor viable. It would be, however, equally unwise for industry to maintain the status quo.

Lisa Stark: It's partly that threat that is motivating change. Tomorrow, the Grocery Manufacturers Association will announce stricter voluntary guidelines, restricting product placements on children's TV shows.

Richard Martin: It's less about external pressures. And it's more about being responsive to consumers.

Lisa Stark: But consumer groups say with children being bombarded by $10 billion in food advertising a year, that it's time for the government to crack down. That self-regulation alone won't work.

Margo Wootan: There has to be pressure on the companies in order to get them to do it. They're not doing this for altruistic reasons.

Lisa Stark: Companies stress that ultimately, it's up to children and parents to choose what they eat. Remember those Red Lobster healthy meals? Only one child out of five orders the vegetables. Lisa Stark, ABC News, Houston.

NOTES

NOTES

NOTES

NOTES

NOTES

NOTES

NOTES

NOTES

NOTES

NOTES

NOTES

NOTES